Boulevard

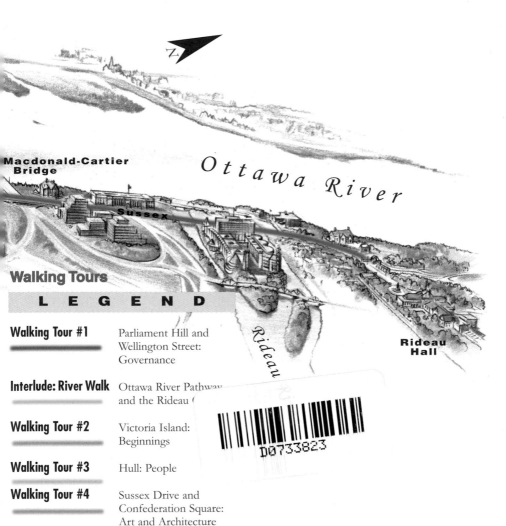

Macdonald-Cartier
Bridge

Ottawa River

Sussex

Rideau

Rideau
Hall

Walking Tours

L E G E N D

CAPITAL INFOCENTRE, starting point
for a Capital Adventure

D0733823

Welcome to
A CAPITAL ADVENTURE

et ready to discover a Capital like no other. This is Canada's Capital Region, a place defined by rivers and dramatic escarpments. Its waterways are lined with sweeping parkways, its core filled with exuberant architecture and living heritage. Canada's Capital Region is thousands of square kilometres in area, and every inch of it brims with excitement and interest.

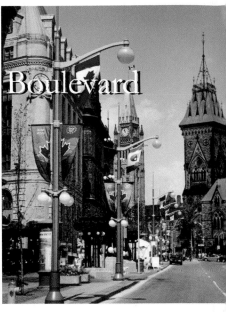

Confederation Boulevard

is the Capital's ceremonial and discovery route, and your avenue to discovering this extraordinary place. The Boulevard runs right through the heart of the Capital and encircles the downtown areas of Ottawa and Hull in one continuous, flag-lined promenade. Along its length lie some of Canada's most important institutions, heritage sites, monuments and festival plazas. Confederation Boulevard offers a pleasant day of strolling and sightseeing with spectacular views and refreshing intervals of contact with nature right in the heart of the city.

Capital Parkways

But don't stop there. Get into your car and explore the treasures that lie outside the core. Visit the outlying museums and institutions that helped to create Canada. Follow the parkways into an experience of Canada's natural and rural heritage. Get to know Canada through its Capital.

Get ready for a Capital Adventure!

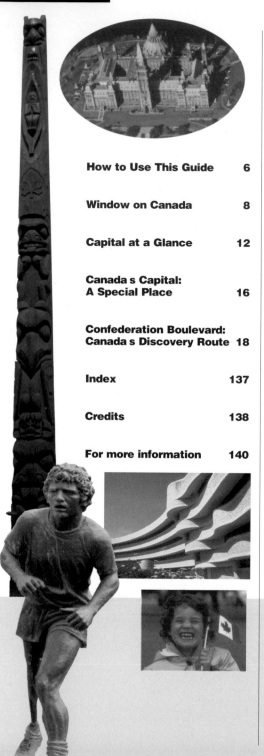

Confederation Boulevard
WALKING TOURS

**1 Parliament Hill
and Wellington Street   20**

Governance

The buildings in this part of the
Capital – including the Parliament
Buildings, the Supreme Court and the
Bank of Canada – are fundamental to
Canada. Historically, legally, economi-
cally and culturally, they shape Canada,
and it is here that much of the work of
government takes place.

Interlude: River Walk
**Ottawa River Pathway and the
Rideau Canal   38**

Consider strolling
along the river for a
half hour or so. Few
cities in the world
have riverbanks so
unspoiled that wanderers only a few
steps from the downtown can still
enjoy a sense of contact with nature.

2 Victoria Island   48

Beginnings

Many of the separate threads of
Canadian history come together at the
Chaudière Falls. Traces of the past are
still visible in the buildings, in the
smokestacks and on grassy slopes
where peoples of the past landed their
canoes, piled their lumber and built
their shops and mills.

3 City of Hull   56

People

From earliest days, Hull has been a
community teeming with life and alive
with sound, whether it's the shriek of
yesterday's industry or the sights and
sounds of the new Canadian Museum
of Civilization. The city has grown,
modernized and diversified without
losing its early hardiness and energy.

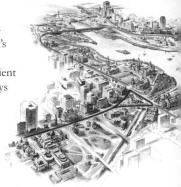

How to

This guide is your key to a Capital adventure! It takes you right around Confederation Boulevard – Canada's Discovery Route – introducing you to major Canadian attractions en route. Then it's off into the larger region on a series of driving tours on the Capital's marvellous scenic parkways. This guide is your convenient three-season companion to exploring the Capital. Some parkways and pathways are closed in winter.

Getting started

BEGIN YOUR CAPITAL ADVENTURE BY GETTING PREPARED

Visit the **National Capital Commission Capital Infocentre** across from Parliament Hill or call us at 239-5000 (open 7 days week) for all the maps, brochures and attractions information you will need to start your visit off right. See pages 140 and 141 for more details on the NCC's information services.

THE CAPITAL ON FOOT

Walking Tours

Confederation Boulevard has been divided into six walking tours, each with its own particular theme, that take you through the heart of the Capital. Or, if you're longing for a peaceful interlude in a busy schedule, follow our directions for a stroll along the Ottawa River.

- Each sector is colour-coded for easy reference.
- Suggested routes guide you around Confederation Boulevard.
- Directions From Your Guide give you useful advice along the way.
- *Sites at a Glance* shows you what you ll see on your tour.
- Eye-catching icons show you what to look for:

 Focus on Canada

 Canadian Profiles

Behind the Scenes

A BIRD S EYE VIEW ▲

Each walking tour features a fantastic map – a coloured bird's eye view – that puts you right in the picture. A legend of sites is numbered and keyed to the map and to stories in the following pages.

CAPITAL STORIES

Bright images combine with lively stories of the Capital, past and present, to bring the region to life.

IN FOCUS

The guide puts the Capital "In Focus" as it zooms in to take you deeper into your experience of the Capital.

THE CAPITAL BY CAR

Driving Tours

Go further out into Canada's Capital Region. Images and stories tell you what to look for *en route*.

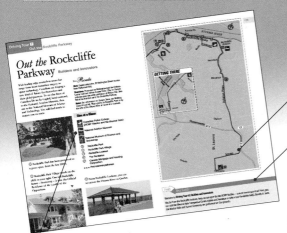

■ Schematic maps with suggested routes are keyed to attractions *en route*.

■ From Your Guide is your handy navigator.

■ Pictograms on the map correspond to signs on the road and lead to national attractions.

See the back inside cover for a complete list.

From

Your Guide

Look for me,
Your Guide, to keep you on track.

Window on Canada

The Nation

A Capital is a reflection of the country it represents. Let us tell you about Canada.

Land of giants

Canada is a huge country, 10 million square kilometres (nearly 4 million square miles) in extent. That makes it one of the world's largest countries, second only to the Russian Federation.

Unspoiled wilderness

Fly over Canada in an airplane – still the only way that you can reach many Canadian towns – and you will see below you an immense, unsettled landscape lined with rivers and scored with thousands of lakes. The oldest rocks in the Canadian Shield, an ancient mountain range that covers close to half of Canada, are nearly four billion years old and were part of the earth's first crust.

Constitutional monarchy

Canada, with its Parliament, is one of the world's great democracies. The Head of State is Queen Elizabeth II. She is represented in Canada by the Governor General – currently Her Excellency the Right Honourable Adrienne Clarkson – whose Official Residence is one of the Capital's most historic houses.

Rights and freedoms

The *Charter of Rights and Freedoms* was written into the *Constitution Act* of 1982. The Charter offers us freedoms and enshrines our rights. We have freedom of association and assembly, freedom of thought, conscience and religion, and freedom of the press.

A federal democracy

Ottawa is the Capital of a federation of ten provinces and three territories, each with its own Capital. The Prime Minister is the elected head of government.

A nation linked to the world

Canada is a trading nation with strong outward links to the world. A country that has been a colony both of France and Britain in its time, today Canada is a fully independent nation, a founding member of the United Nations and a member of both the Commonwealth of Nations (a legacy of the British Empire) and La francophonie (an International Cooperation Society of French-speaking nations formed in 1970).

1000
Norse sailors under Lief Ericsson land in what is now Newfoundland

1497
John Cabot claims the northeastern Atlantic Coast for England

15,000 to 20,000 years ago
The first peoples make their way across the landscape.

1400

1450

■ How did Canada get its name? The Aboriginal word "kanata" actually meant "village," but 16th-century European map-makers used it to describe all the land north of the St. Lawrence River.

■ Canada is a huge country extending 4,500 kilometres (2,796 miles) from north to south and even further from east to west. It is comparable in size to the whole of Europe.

The Yukon

Territories

Northwest Territories

Nunavut

Provinces

British Columbia

Alberta

Saskatchewan

Manitoba

Ontario

Quebec

Newfoundland and Labrador

Prince Edward Island

Nova Scotia

New Brunswick

■ Canada and the United States share the longest undefended border in the world – 8,890 kilometres (5,525 miles) long.

■ The world's longest national highway is the Trans-Canada, which runs 7,699 kilometres (4,784 miles) from St. John's, Newfoundland, to Victoria, British Columbia (coast to coast).

1535
Jacques Cartier explores the St. Lawrence River as far as present-day Montreal

Port Royal

1605
The French establish Port Royal – only the second permanent settlement in North America – in what is now Nova Scotia

1642
Montreal is founded

1500   1550   1600   1650   1700

Window *on Canada*

The People

Canada has been a nation since 1867, the year that Confederation bound together a number of separate British colonies in northeastern North America. That's not long – a little more than 13 decades or the length of some five generations. Canada's Aboriginal peoples take the story thousands of years further back in time.

Primeval roots

For many thousands of years before Europeans first set foot on Canadian soil (a thousand years ago) or claimed the first fragment of Canadian coastline as their own (500 years), Aboriginal inhabitants hunted, traded and built their villages on the lakes and waterways of this harsh northern land.

The age of settlement

Europeans arrived in the late 15th century, and the country gradually opened up to exploration and trade. The years passed, and more immigrants from Europe and the United States came here, carved their farms out of the wilderness and pushed railways into the west. Together, they created a new Canada that stretched from coast to coast.

Today's reality

Canada is one of the world's most socially diverse and peaceful nations. Canadians are a truly global collective. "Old" Canadians of Aboriginal, British and French origin have been joined in recent years by "new" Canadians from every region on earth.

John A. Macdonald

New Westminster, BC   *Government House, PEI*

1867
Four British colonies –
New Brunswick, Nova
Scotia, Quebec and
Ontario – unite to
create Canada

1870
Canada explodes
westward with the
purchase of Manitoba
and the Northwest
Territories from the
Hudson's Bay Company

1871
British Columbia joins
Canada, on condition
that a railway be driven
through from east
to west

1873
Prince Edward Island,
tiny but one of the
richest agricultural
regions of northeastern
North America,
joins Canada

1885
The last spike of
trans-continenta
railway is driven
Canada is linked
from coast to coa
by a ribbon of ste

1850

Though 70 percent of the Canadian landscape is wilderness – with no trace of human settlement – two-thirds of Canadians live in cities (half of those in Montreal, Toronto and Vancouver).

For over five years now, the United Nations has declared Canada the world's best place to live.

Canadians now speak 100 languages as their mother tongue, with English and French predominating (16.9 million English-speaking Canadians and 6.6 million French in the 1990s, with Italian, German and Chinese coming next).

More than one million Canadians claim native ancestry.

Canada has more trees than people. In 2000, there were an estimated 30.7 million Canadians — about one-fiftieth the population of China and one-tenth that of the United States. What they lack in numbers, Canadians make up in diversity. Population growth in today's Canada — about a million people in the 1990s — comes mainly from immigration.

Gold Rush

Newfoundland outport

1898
The Yukon, at the height of the Gold Rush, is made into a separate territory

1905
Alberta and Saskatchewan are carved out of the Northwest Territories and created as provinces

1949
Newfoundland becomes the last Canadian province to join Canada

1967
Canada celebrates its Centennial and a hundred years of nationhood

1999
Nunavut, largely inhabited by Inuit, is established as a territory in its own right

1900 *1950* *2000*

Capital at a Glance

From Wilderness to Modern Capital

Encompassing thousands of square kilometres of city, field, forest, moor and mountain, Canada's Capital Region is a microcosm of Canada. And, like much of Canada, the Capital Region is defined by its waterways – the Ottawa, Gatineau and Rideau rivers, which come together in the shadow of Parliament Hill. Along the south shore of the Ottawa River, the water has cut deeply into soft, sedimentary limestone to create a series of dramatic escarpments. Northward, the hard granite edge of the Laurentian Highlands forms a second long escarpment (the boundary of Gatineau Park).

First peoples

The first sign of human activity in northern North America dates back some 20,000 years, when migrants from Asia are believed to have made their way across a temporary land bridge in what is now the Bering Sea. By the time European explorers sailed west in the 15th century, these peoples and their descendants had filtered into every part of the Western Hemisphere, creating civilizations far to the south and developing many different cultures and languages.

Exploration

In 1610, a European traveller – a young Frenchman by the name of Étienne Brûlé – travelled up the forested river valley where Ottawa and Hull now stand and discovered a new world. In his footsteps, generation after generation of explorers and traders came up the Ottawa River.

Explorer Samuel de Champlain and Aboriginal guides ▲

The fur trade

Every spring from the 16th to the 19th centuries, great brigades of trading canoes came surging up the Ottawa on their way from Montreal to the far west. The "voyageurs" – meaning "travellers" in French – carried guns and cloth and metal tools on their annual pilgrimage into the wilderness and traded them to Aboriginal peoples in exchange for rich cargoes of fur.

Settlement

Settlement did not reach the Ottawa Valley until 1800, when a party of Americans came upriver by sleigh in search of farmland. A few years later, the British army arrived with orders to build a canal through the wilderness. In their wake came a flood of immigration. Hull, though originally settled by English-speaking immigrants, is now predominantly French, with 83 percent of its residents speaking French as their mother tongue. Ottawa was settled originally by French-Canadian, Scottish and Irish workers in the early 1800s, with later waves of settlement arriving from Britain, the United States and parts of Europe and the Middle East.

Creating a Capital

In 1857, Queen Victoria accepted the advice of her Canadian counsellors and chose a remote little lumber town called Ottawa as the new Capital of the Province of Canada. Ottawa, which lay on the border of two provinces in a location of great beauty, was an inspired choice.

Queen Victoria (reigned 1837-1901)

Parliament Buildings under construction, 1860s

Capital at a Glance

A Bird's Eye View

Pretend that you are leaning over the edge of the wickerwork basket and looking down. The impression you'd get would be *greenness*. There are parks everywhere in Canada's Capital Region – lining the waterways, breaking up the grey pattern of buildings and threaded like green beads along Confederation Boulevard. To the northwest lies the huge expanse of Gatineau Park – 35,600 hectares (88,000 acres) of rocky, forested land at the steep edge of the Canadian Shield. Southward, the Greenbelt throws a wide band of protected wild and rural land around the city. Canada's Capital deserves its nickname – the "Green Capital."

Imagine yourself floating over the Capital in a huge, brightly coloured hot-air balloon.

The living past

The past is a living presence here. You can feel it. In the Parliament Buildings, possibly the finest example of Victorian exuberance in the world, Canadian heritage has crystallized into patterns of stone and glass.

Capital waterways

Canada's Capital is a place where the waters meet. The Ottawa River runs like a broad silver ribbon through the heart of the region, dividing Ontario from Quebec. Into it, from the north and south respectively, flow the Gatineau and Rideau rivers. These waterways, with the Rideau Canal, define the shape and character of the land.

Colourful hot air balloons fill the air over the Capital when the Gatineau Hot Air Balloon Festival takes place each year in September.

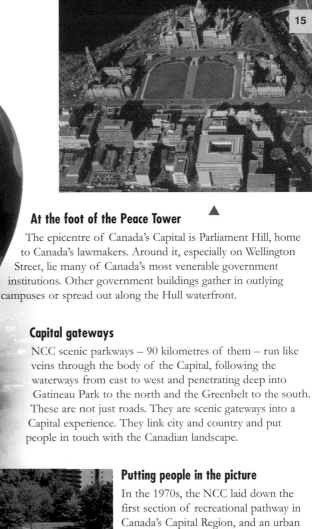

At the foot of the Peace Tower

The epicentre of Canada's Capital is Parliament Hill, home to Canada's lawmakers. Around it, especially on Wellington Street, lie many of Canada's most venerable government institutions. Other government buildings gather in outlying campuses or spread out along the Hull waterfront.

Capital gateways

NCC scenic parkways – 90 kilometres of them – run like veins through the body of the Capital, following the waterways from east to west and penetrating deep into Gatineau Park to the north and the Greenbelt to the south. These are not just roads. They are scenic gateways into a Capital experience. They link city and country and put people in touch with the Canadian landscape.

Putting people in the picture

In the 1970s, the NCC laid down the first section of recreational pathway in Canada's Capital Region, and an urban revolution began. Today, cyclists, walkers and in-line skaters enjoy a network of more than 150 kilometres (93 miles) of pathways. This system links the Capital, through the 15,000-kilometre (9,321-mile) Trans Canada Trail, to the whole of Canada.

A century of painstaking work

Canada's Capital is no accident. It is the result of more than a century of painstaking planning that began with the creation of the Ottawa Improvement Commission (ancestor of today's National Capital Commission – NCC) in 1899. Since then, successive plans have laid out an extraordinary network of parks, pathways and parkways for miles around Parliament Hill – the jewel of the Capital.

Canada's Capital
A Special Place

This is a Capital for all Canadians, a place that matters, a home away from home. As you set off to discover the Capital, remember that you are, in effect, exploring Canada.

Canada's meeting place

The Capital of a great country is many things, not least of all a national gathering place. Every year, millions of Canadians come to this Capital on business or holiday. They bring their children here to see Canadian pageantry and to learn about being Canadian. On Canada Day, they join in huge festive crowds on Parliament Hill and in the Capital's parks. They gather in silent respect at the National War Memorial on Remembrance Day. At every time of year they wander the museums in search of Canada. Think about this and more as you explore the Capital, a place like no other.

Seat of government

Here in the Capital, laws are made, policies shaped and decisions taken that affect the lives of Canadians in countless direct and immediate ways.

Canadian government at work

Not for nothing are they called "public servants." They labour here in the Capital, where many federal departments are headquartered, to deliver the services that Canadians need and deserve.

Canada's treasure houses

Canadian Museum of Civilization

Countless priceless artifacts of Canadian heritage are stored, safeguarded and made available to Canadians in the Capital's national museums.

National addresses

You know their faces from newspapers and television. They live here in the Capital, in Official Residences that house the Governor General, the Prime Minister and other prominent Canadians.

24 Sussex Drive, Official Residence of the Prime Minister

A place of ceremony

Canadians gather in the Capital to participate in moments of pageantry or national sorrow, as in the sombre annual ritual of Remembrance Day. ▶

The international Capital

It is here that Canada meets the world. More than a hundred foreign countries send their representatives to Canada's Capital Region, and dozens of institutions work to shape Canada's place on the international stage.

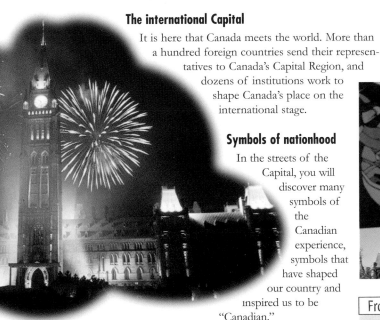

Symbols of nationhood

In the streets of the Capital, you will discover many symbols of the Canadian experience, symbols that have shaped our country and inspired us to be "Canadian."

A place of celebration

Being part of a crowd of thousands on Parliament Hill on Canada Day (July 1) is an experience that really lets you know what it means to be Canadian. This is only one of a series of national celebrations that mark the year in Canada's Capital.

From ▷ Your Guide

Much of what makes this Capital so unique and special is found on Confederation Boulevard. Turn the page to discover more.

Confederation Boulevard

Canada's Discovery Route

Confederation Boulevard is the Capital's ceremonial route. It is also Canada's Discovery Route. Follow Confederation Boulevard, discover the Capital and get to know Canada.

Confederation Boulevard is the place to start your exploration of Canada's Capital Region. This award-winning Boulevard is a microcosm of Canada. Lined with some of Canada's most important national institutions, including Parliament and the Supreme Court of Canada, it is also home to some of Canada's foremost cultural institutions – for example, the National Gallery of Canada and the Canadian Museum of Civilization. And it is the site of pride-inspiring commemorations such as the National War Memorial and the Peacekeeping Monument.

A few facts:

- Confederation Boulevard includes parts of five streets (Wellington, Elgin, Mackenzie and Laurier streets and Sussex Drive) and two provinces (Ontario and Quebec), as well as two bridges (Portage and Alexandra) spanning the Ottawa River.

- Confederation Boulevard is based on the traditional ceremonial route connecting the Governor General's and Prime Minister's residences with Parliament Hill.

- When the Capital hosts a foreign dignitary, the visiting nation's flag is flown along the ceremonial route.

- Over the years, salt and other pollutants have killed many of the fine old trees that once lined Confederation Boulevard. Planning teams now choose species of trees known for their urban hardiness. Underground root chambers and watering systems help as well.

- Confederation Boulevard boasts an award-winning urban design.

How you know you're there

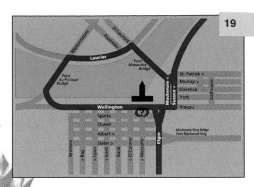

Look around you. Do you see broad, tree-lined sidewalks edged with red granite and tall, banner-festooned lampposts? If so, you are on Confederation Boulevard. Look for these features to stay on track.

Lighting the way

Follow the maple leaf. On the "Crown" side of the boulevard, tall, distinctive lampposts are crowned with gleaming bronze leaves. They mark your route along Canada's ceremonial route.

Trees

Some of the oldest sections of the Boulevard are lined with mature maples. The newer parts have been planted with beautiful linden trees.

Canadian granite

What could be more Canadian? The red speckled granite that is used for curbs and cobblestones on Confederation Boulevard comes from the Canadian Shield.

Signage

Confederation Boulevard is an amalgamation of several existing streets. It may sound confusing, but you can't mistake it. The street signs, all in signature red and green, are crowned with the characteristic maple leaf.

PROM. **SUSSEX** DR.

From

Your Guide

Now you know what we mean by "Confederation Boulevard." You're ready to begin the adventure. Remember, look for me, your guide, to keep you on track.

Banners and flags

All summer, the Boulevard is lined with colourful banners that mark and commemorate special events in the life of the nation and of the world.

Looking for information?

INFORMATION KIOSKS

If it's information you need, look for these large kiosks, each topped with a maple leaf and finished in Confederation Boulevard colours. They stand at key intersections.

Parliament Hill and Wellington Street

The deep roots, civility and strength of Canadian democracy are expressed in the majestic buildings on Parliament Hill and Wellington Street

You are standing on Wellington Street, an important part of Confederation Boulevard. Here, in the majestic buildings that line both sides of the street, the work of governing takes place. Parliament Hill, possibly the world's most exuberant expression of Victorian energy and romance, is the jewel on Confederation Boulevard. But it is only one of an array of nation-building institutions in this sector. The Bank of Canada, the Supreme Court, the National Archives of Canada – these are among the institutions that shape Canada. Take your time exploring them.

① The Capital Infocentre

This is more than an information centre – it's a visitor experience in itself. Spend some time looking at a scale model of the Capital, spinning through the Capital on a brisk cinematic tour and enjoying the Capital's most spectacular view of Parliament Hill.

Sites at a Glance

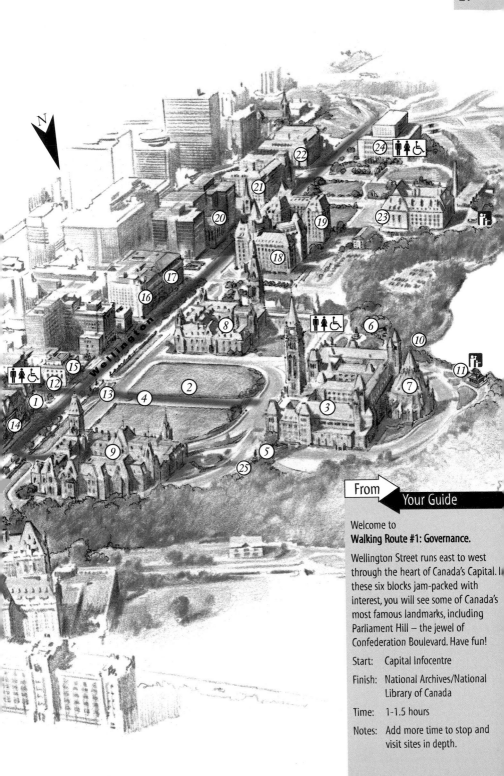

From **Your Guide**

Welcome to
Walking Route #1: Governance.

Wellington Street runs east to west through the heart of Canada's Capital. I these six blocks jam-packed with interest, you will see some of Canada's most famous landmarks, including Parliament Hill – the jewel of Confederation Boulevard. Have fun!

Start: Capital Infocentre

Finish: National Archives/National Library of Canada

Time: 1-1.5 hours

Notes: Add more time to stop and visit sites in depth.

Welcome to Parliament Hill

Barracks Hill ▲

Parliament Hill (in the upper right of this image) was a military barracks before it was a centre of government. British soldiers came into the wilderness in 1826 and chose this hill as the perfect site for fortifications.

② Canada's Meeting Place

Parliament Hill – the single most recognizable landmark in Canada – embodies many of the values that Canadians are most proud of – democracy, tolerance and freedom of speech. It is the workplace of parliamentarians and their staff, but it is also the home of all Canadians. One of only four Gothic capitals in the world – the others are London, Budapest and Pretoria – Ottawa offers an extraordinary experience of architectural splendour. Three buildings stand on Parliament Hill – the Centre Block, the East Block (on your right as you face the Centre Block) and the West Block. Get up close, and you will see gargoyles and grotesques of every size and shape carved into the walls. Hard to believe, but the arm-like projections at the top of the Peace Tower are eight feet long!

Tower, original Centre Block

Phoenix from the Ashes

On the night of February 3, 1916, fire began in the Centre Block. The cause is unknown – an overturned lamp, cigar ash or even the work of wartime saboteurs? Within hours, the Centre Block was a giant torch. Thanks to the quick action of a parliamentary employee, fireproof doors were slammed shut, and the

③ Centre Block

Victorian Exuberance

From Your Guide

Stay on the Hill for more interesting stories.

By Joseph Sheard, in the Tudor spirit, 1859

A parliamentary "might have been"

In 1859, architects competed to design Canada's new legislature. This is one of 32 designs that were submitted. As you can see, Parliament Hill might have looked very different.

Prince in the wilderness

Edward, Prince of Wales – the young and dashing son of Queen Victoria (left) – made history in 1860 as the first member of the Royal Family to visit North America. With great pomp and ceremony, he laid the cornerstone of the Centre Block (far left). After the 1916 fire, the stone was dug out of the rubble and relaid at the southeast corner of the Peace Tower where you can see it today.

Library of Parliament was saved. From Parliament Hill, you can look straight down Metcalfe Street and see the Victoria Memorial Museum in the distance. There, Parliament reconvened on the day after the fire, and there it stayed while the Centre Block was rebuilt. Today, the Victoria Memorial Museum houses the Canadian Museum of Nature (see page 112).

On Parliament Hill

Symbols of Canada

The Flag Debate

What travelling Canadian has not felt proud to catch a glimpse of the Canadian flag in some faraway place? Astonishingly, until 1965, Canada had no official flag of its own. Our present flag – red and white with the maple leaf in the centre – was just one of many designs that Parliament debated and people protested in the 1960s. After some 250 impassioned speeches – the most speeches on any subject ever in the House of Commons – members voted on December 15, 1964 at 2 o'clock in the morning. The motion carried, 163 to 78. Canada's new flag was raised for the first time on the Peace Tower on February 15, 1965.

The Maple Leaf

The sign of the maple leaf, now recognized all over the world as the "Canadian" symbol, was incorporated into the Coat of Arms in 1921. The maple leaf was recognized in Quebec as an unofficial emblem as early as 1700 and came into widespread popular use in 1867, when Alexander Muir wrote "The Maple Leaf Forever," for many years Canada's unofficial anthem.

Speaking of Canada

Canada was granted a Coat of Arms in 1921 showing the symbols of Canada's European founders – the French *fleur de lis*, the English lions, the Scottish lion and the Irish harp. Look for them carved in stone outside the main doorway of the Centre Block.

④ An undying light

In 1967, Canada celebrated 100 years of
Confederation, and Prime Minister Pearson lit the
Centennial Flame on Parliament Hill. Intended as
a temporary part of the year-long celebrations,
it has since become an "eternal" flame.

Newfoundland coat of arms

⑤ *Sir John A. Macdonald*

⑥ *Sir George-Étienne Cartier (inset)*

The meeting of East and West

There are two statues on Parliament Hill you should be sure to
look at. They honour two men who, more than any others,
created Canada: Sir John A. Macdonald, a small-town lawyer
who took to politics in 1843, when Ontario was still called
Canada West; and Sir George-Étienne Cartier, the best
known and most highly respected politician of his
generation in Canada East (Quebec). The political union
that Macdonald and Cartier forged as co-premiers of the
Province of Canada from 1857 to 1862 laid the
foundation for Confederation. Their determination,
oratory and political savvy did the rest.

These are just two of the
interesting statues on
Parliament Hill. For a
comprehensive guide to them, pick up your free copy of
Discover the Hill, available year-round at the NCC Capital
Infocentre (across Wellington Street) or during the summer
at the InfoTent on the Hill.

From Your Guide

Keep going!
There's still more to come on
Canada's Parliament Buildings!

Parliament Hill: *A Treasure to Explore*

Experience it by visiting the
Public Works and Government Services Canada website.

Go to: **www.parliamenthill.gc.ca**

Public Works and Government Services Canada

Travaux publics et Services gouvernementaux Canada

Canadä

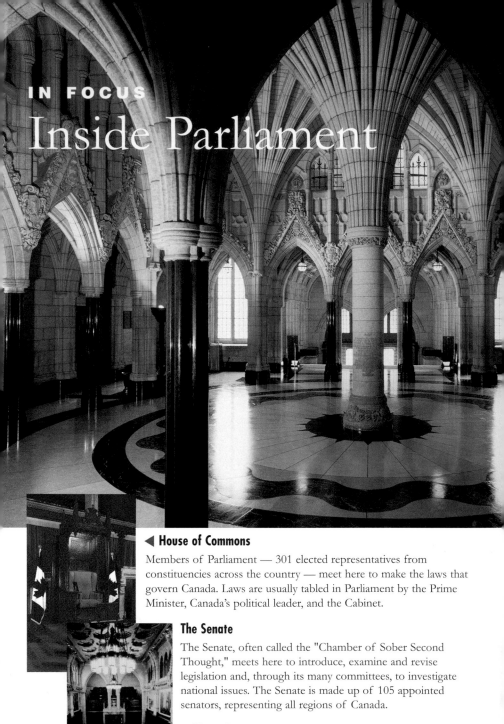

Inside Parliament

◀ House of Commons

Members of Parliament — 301 elected representatives from
constituencies across the country — meet here to make the laws that
govern Canada. Laws are usually tabled in Parliament by the Prime
Minister, Canada's political leader, and the Cabinet.

The Senate

The Senate, often called the "Chamber of Sober Second
Thought," meets here to introduce, examine and revise
legislation and, through its many committees, to investigate
national issues. The Senate is made up of 105 appointed
senators, representing all regions of Canada.

Public Galleries

Every day when the Senate or the House of Commons is
sitting, the public galleries — banks of seats at the end of each
chamber — are open to anyone who wants to watch the
business of state being conducted.

Memorial Chapel

If a Canadian family lost someone during the war, it can take comfort in the fact that his or her name is recorded forever in one of the Books of Remembrance in the Peace Tower. Every day, pages of these books are turned in a solemn, private ceremony. Families may attend, subject to prior arrangement.

⑦ The Library of Parliament

The iron structure of the Library of Parliament's dome was assembled in England and shipped whole to Canada. Unfortunately, the measurements were off, and back the dome went – not once, but twice – for adjustments. The Library was completed in 1876 and survived two fires, one in 1916 and another in 1952.

Long into the night

With many responsibilities outside of the Senate and House of Commons chambers, Parliamentarians' busy schedules include legislative committee work, meeting with Canadians, media interviews and political functions. A Parliamentarian's workday does not end at 5 pm; in fact, it can go long into the night. On December 9, 1999, for example, the House of Commons considered the proposed Nisga'a treaty for 43 consecutive hours. When Parliament is sitting, parliamentary and Library staff, administrators and trades-people are all on hand to serve Parliament behind the scenes.

The Carillon ▲

On July 1, 1927, a ring of 53 bells was inaugurated in the Peace Tower. That same day, the sound of the Carillon was broadcast nationally, one of the earliest sounds to reach into every corner of Canada via the magic of radio. Throughout the year, carillon concerts are held most days at noon, and at 2 p.m. in July and August.

History in stone

Eleanor Milne, sculptor, is just one of generations of stone carvers who have left their mark on the Parliament Buildings. From 1964 to 1975, she worked nightly on scaffolding to carve the History of Canada frieze in the House of Commons Foyer. ▼

From Your Guide

You're ready now to leave the Hill and to explore the rest of the Parliamentary Precinct. Just head down to Wellington Street, turn right and walk along the north side of the street to continue the adventure.

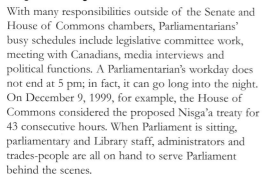

Wellington Street, 1853

Visions of grandeur

In the old days, Wellington Street was nothing more than a broad expanse of dirt, with cows and pigs wandering along the grassy verge. However, Colonel John By of the Royal Engineers – who ordered the street to be laid out in the 1820s – saw beyond the town's rough pioneer beginnings and insisted that Wellington Street should be made broad enough to serve as a city boulevard some day. The street was named for the Duke of Wellington, commander of the British forces that defeated Napoleon at Waterloo in 1815.

Wellington Street
Named for "The Iron Duke"

⑭ Moving off the Hill
Langevin Building

Canada's civil service soon outgrew its quarters on Parliament Hill and the Langevin Building was erected across the street (1883-89). Since the days of Pierre Trudeau, the prime minister of Canada has had his office in the Langevin Block. The building was designed by the same architect who designed the Parliament Buildings, and it was named for Hector-Louis Langevin, former Mayor of Quebec City and Father of Confederation.

Constant Penency, Algonquin

An Aboriginal like the one figured above, Constant Penency fought for the British in the War of 1812. In a petition dictated in 1830, he explained how settlement was ruining his livelihood. "After several years the hunt has more and more diminished with the destruction and the distancing of beaver and game." Penency finished his days half a century later as a pensioner of the British government.

⑲ Justice Building ▲

Built in 1935-38, at the height of the Depression, the Justice Building nevertheless carried forward the Gothic theme, expressing the dignity and majesty of government. Notice the fine carving of the voyageur (fur-trader) and an Aboriginal on the west-facing facade.

◀ ⑯ Our right to know

Canadians have a direct line to events in Parliament, which are monitored daily by journalists representing wire services and newspapers from all over Canada and headquartered in the National Press Building.

⑫ and ⑬ Profiles in Courage ★ ★

⑫ Terry Fox is one of Canada's most recognized and beloved heroes. In 1980, Fox, who had lost a leg to cancer, began a cross-country run to raise money for cancer research. Canadians were drawn by his determination. A recurrence of the cancer cut short his run, but his courage inspired a nation. The courage of another young Canadian, Henry Albert Harper, who threw himself into the frozen water of the Ottawa River in an effort to save a young woman, is commemorated by the statue of ⑬ Sir Galahad.

Wellington Street continued

⑰ Wellington Building

The Canadian Coat of Arms is carved into the facade of this grand edifice. Once the Canadian head office of the Metropolitan Life Insurance Company, the building now houses offices of Members of Parliament, including the Leader of the Opposition. Stop and look at the Byzantine-style mosaic in the lobby, showing the Met as the Great Mother with policy-holders and employees at her feet.

㉑ Church and State

St Andrew's has been the site of much pomp and ceremony over the years. On one occasion in 1943, a Dutch princess – the child of parents who fled their country during war – was christened here, with Queen Mary of England and President Roosevelt of the United States acting as godparents in absentia.

⑱ Confederation Building

T. W. Fuller, son of the man who designed the Centre Block, was Chief Architect of Public Works in 1927, when work began on the Confederation Building, and he helped ensure the spread of Neo-Gothic – fast becoming a kind of "national" style – along Wellington Street.

㉑ St. Andrew's Church

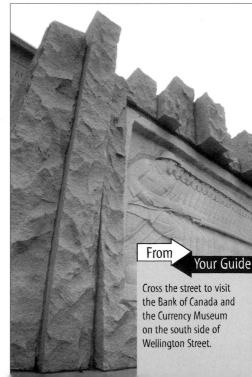

㉒ In Memoriam

"The Canadian Phalanx," by sculptor Ivan Meštrovic, was carved after the First World War to honour Canada's veterans. The buildings connected by the Memorial Arch were originally occupied by the departments of Veterans Affairs (on the left) and Trade and Commerce.

From Your Guide

Cross the street to visit the Bank of Canada and the Currency Museum on the south side of Wellington Street.

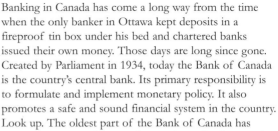

⑳ Bank of Canada

Governing Canada's Wealth

Step through the doors of the old bank, into the marble hall, and you'll think you've returned to classical antiquity

Canada's central bank

Banking in Canada has come a long way from the time when the only banker in Ottawa kept deposits in a fireproof tin box under his bed and chartered banks issued their own money. Those days are long since gone. Created by Parliament in 1934, today the Bank of Canada is the country's central bank. Its primary responsibility is to formulate and implement monetary policy. It also promotes a safe and sound financial system in the country. Look up. The oldest part of the Bank of Canada has seven bronze plaques above the door, each representing one of Canada's founding industries – they are fishing, hydro-electricity, mining, farming, forestry, manufacturing and building.

Ottawa headquarters

The granite block of the original Bank (1937) is now wrapped in modern glass towers (1972-79) to create a striking melding of old and new. Step through the doors of the old bank, into the marble hall, and you'll think you've returned to classical antiquity.

On another note

As the federal government's banker, the Bank of Canada also designs and issues new bank notes – though not at this site – incorporating various protections against counterfeiting. It supplies them to financial institutions and destroys notes no longer fit for circulation.

The Currency Museum

Money in Context
The Currency Museum is located in the Bank of Canada — enter via Sparks Street.

Against the backdrop of time

Money is just money until you look at it in context. Then it becomes history. The Currency Museum is a pioneer in presenting the tangled story of currency against a backdrop of history from ancient China to today. Consider Canada – a colonial outpost for many years. Some strange things once passed for money in this country – playing cards with an IOU scribbled by the governor or brass buttons flattened to resemble halfpennies.

All for love

Coins often tell a story. Take Wallis Simpson, for example. She changed the face of Canadian coinage when King Edward VIII abdicated for love of her in 1936. The timing, just as the next year's coins were being prepared, was unfortunate. Without time to redesign the issue, a tiny dot was added to certain coins to mark the ones that, though they bore the face of Edward's father, actually belonged to the reign of his younger brother, George VI. Such coins are rare relics of a moment in time.

Early Canadian coinage, five-cent piece, 1870

A treasure trove

Researchers, collectors and anyone interested in coins and notes will find them out in the open here, not sealed away in a vault. This museum has the largest collection of Canadian coins, tokens and bank notes anywhere, and many of them are on display.

For kids

Watch out for counterfeits! Test your eye on an array of genuine and false notes. Children who get a kick out of this may also like to dress up in the costumes of the ages — in a Roman toga or a royal dress — and pose as the effigy on a coin. This is just part of an array of intriguing children's activities.

For more information see ad on page 134.

From ▸ **Your Guide**

Go back to the north side of Wellington Street and continue walking westward.

Supreme Court of Canada

Majesty of the Law

These broad steps, guarded by the massively draped figures of Truth and Justice, lead through giant doors into a world of lofty spaces and gleaming marble that perfectly represents the majesty of the law.

㉓ Highest Court in the land

This is a place of intense gravity. There is a hush in the grey marbled corridors of the Supreme Court of Canada and in reading rooms where 400 year old legal books line the walls. Since 1949, Canadians have come here as the court of final appeal. Nine justices deliberate on points of law and interpret and rule on legal issues that are vital to Canadians. When both flagpoles are flying Canadian flags, Court is in session and you are welcome to attend.

Searching for Truth and Justice

In the 1920s, Walter S. Allward was asked to sculpt the memorial to Canadian soldiers in Vimy, France. Hastily crating up his current work – twin statues of Truth and Justice – he headed for France. Somehow the statues got lost after that, only to be rediscovered in 1969. Today, they stand where they belong, in front of the Supreme Court.

VERITAS

Today the Court has nine members. From left to right: Frank Iacobucci, Louise Arbour, Claire L'Heureux-Dubé, Michel Bastarache, Beverley McLachlin (Chief Justice), William Ian Corneil Binnie, Charles Doherty Gonthier, Louise LeBel and John C. Major.

About the justices

The Supreme Court consists of the Chief Justice of Canada and eight puisne Justices appointed by the Governor-in-Council. Of the nine, three must, by law, be appointed from Quebec. Traditionally, the federal government appoints three Justices from Ontario, two from the West, and one from Atlantic Canada. At sittings of the Court, the Justices usually appear in black silk robes but they wear their ceremonial robes of bright scarlet trimmed with Canadian white mink in Court on special occasions and in the Senate at the opening of each new session of Parliament. Decisions of the Court need not be unanimous; a majority may decide, with dissenting reasons given by the minority. Each Justice may write reasons in any case if he or she chooses to do so.

Man of the law ⭐

The red robe on display in the foyer of the Supreme Court dates back to the 16th century in style, and it represents the deep roots of Canadian legal tradition. This robe was worn on ceremonial occasions by the Right Honourable Brian Dickson, Chief Justice of Canada from 1984 to 1990. A native of Saskatchewan, he played a key role in interpreting the 1982 *Canadian Charter of Rights and Freedoms*. The Charter was part of the constitutional reform that resulted in the patriation of the Constitution in 1982.

"TEMPORARY" BUILDINGS

To one side of the Supreme Court stands a white frame building, the last of the Capital's so-called "temporary" buildings. This is a relic of an era of history when thousands of civil servants poured into Ottawa to support the war effort in 1939, and offices had to be hastily thrown up.

㉔ National Archives *of* Canada

Preserving Canada's Memory

The raw materials of history 🍁

The sound of microfilm clicking and papers rustling in the large, hushed Reading Room – these are the sounds of Canadian history being mined for its treasures. Canada was only five years old in 1872, when legislators began planning how to preserve Canada's historical records and created the Public Archives. Today, the National Archives' collection includes a vast wealth of maps, diaries, films, journals, architectural drawings, documentary art, official records, photographs, videos, sound recordings and films. These are nothing less than the raw materials of history.

Portals into the past

Step inside the National Archives at 395 Wellington to discover fascinating exhibits. Each is a portal into Canada's past, where hundreds of rare documents tell the diverse stories of our country and its peoples. The permanent exhibit *Treasured Memories* includes precious early maps, photographs, art, diaries and films tracing four centuries of life in Canada. ▼

Gift from the past ⭐

In 1902, Parliament decreed that important records should "be assembled in one place and put in the custody of one person." That person was Arthur Doughty, appointed Dominion Archivist in 1904. Over the next 31 years, he inspired Canadian archivists with the idea of the physical record as the "gift of one generation to another." Doughty is the only civil servant in Ottawa to be honoured with a statue. Go and see it. It sits on the north side of the Archives with a fine view of the river.

Arthur Doughty, at work and (above) captured in bronze

National Library
of Canada   Library for the Nation

Portrait of Canada

Every year from 1632 to 1672, Jesuit missionaries in French Canada wrote detailed reports home to France. The *Jesuit Relations*, which were virtual "bestsellers" in their day, paint a vivid portrait of the life in New France. They were also among the first books on Canada and are a precious part of the vast collection of the National Library of Canada. Since 1953, the National Library has been the single richest source of published works and recordings on all things Canadian. It collects and preserves Canada's published heritage and makes it available to present and future generations of Canadians.

From the library's collection of rare Hebraica

All things Canadian

The collection is hugely varied, everything from the literary manuscripts of Gabrielle Roy and rare Hebraica and Judaica to a copy of Canada's first book on lacrosse, printed just two years after Confederation. In the fields of literature, music, history and genealogy, the National Library's shelves are full of memories, creations, inspirations and interpretations.

Canadian treasures

Glenn Gould's piano, which stands in the Auditorium, still has a part to play in Canadian music. The Library's collection is brought to life throughout the year by concerts, exhibitions and readings.

Service first

Library staff will help you navigate the huge collection and ensure that any question, no matter how difficult or obscure, is answered.

For more information, see the advertisement on page 132.

From Your Guide

You have now completed **Walking Tour #1** and face a decision – whether to head back towards Parliament Hill along the **River Walk** (see next page) or to continue on along Confederation Boulevard to Victoria Island **(Walking Tour #2)** or across the river into Hull **(Walking Tour #3)**. In any case, this is your last chance for a while to stop for washrooms or food and drink (fifth floor).

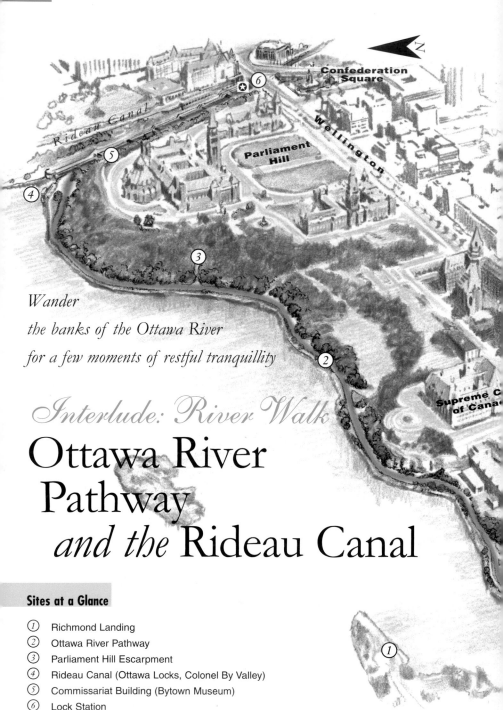

Confederation
Square

Rideau Canal

Wellington

Parliament
Hill

*Wander
the banks of the Ottawa River
for a few moments of restful tranquillity*

Supreme C
of Cana

Interlude: River Walk
Ottawa River Pathway *and the* Rideau Canal

Sites at a Glance

① Richmond Landing
② Ottawa River Pathway
③ Parliament Hill Escarpment
④ Rideau Canal (Ottawa Locks, Colonel By Valley)
⑤ Commissariat Building (Bytown Museum)
⑥ Lock Station
✪ Stairs

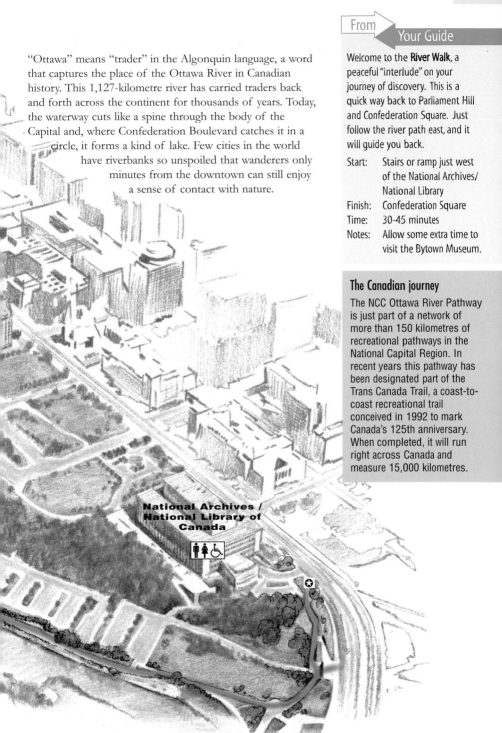

"Ottawa" means "trader" in the Algonquin language, a word that captures the place of the Ottawa River in Canadian history. This 1,127-kilometre river has carried traders back and forth across the continent for thousands of years. Today, the waterway cuts like a spine through the body of the Capital and, where Confederation Boulevard catches it in a circle, it forms a kind of lake. Few cities in the world have riverbanks so unspoiled that wanderers only minutes from the downtown can still enjoy a sense of contact with nature.

From Your Guide

Welcome to the **River Walk**, a peaceful "interlude" on your journey of discovery. This is a quick way back to Parliament Hill and Confederation Square. Just follow the river path east, and it will guide you back.

Start: Stairs or ramp just west of the National Archives/ National Library
Finish: Confederation Square
Time: 30-45 minutes
Notes: Allow some extra time to visit the Bytown Museum.

The Canadian journey

The NCC Ottawa River Pathway is just part of a network of more than 150 kilometres of recreational pathways in the National Capital Region. In recent years this pathway has been designated part of the Trans Canada Trail, a coast-to-coast recreational trail conceived in 1992 to mark Canada's 125th anniversary. When completed, it will run right across Canada and measure 15,000 kilometres.

National Archives / National Library of Canada

The Ottawa River
Wilderness Highway

The Grand River

The Ottawa River is the most important tributary of the St. Lawrence. For much of its length, the Ottawa forms the border between Ontario and Quebec and the boundary between two important land forms – the Canadian Shield and the St. Lawrence Lowlands. An Aboriginal trading route from some 6,000 years ago, the river also proved to be the shortest route for fur-traders paddling from Montreal to the Great Lakes, though it was a tough trip with many rapids and falls and portages. Today the Ottawa and its tributaries have been extensively dammed – including at the Capital's Chaudière Falls – to produce many millions of horsepower from hydro-electricity.

The first geologist

In 1845, a geologist travelled up the Ottawa for the first time, making notes and sketches in a leather-bound notebook (now preserved at the National Archives of Canada).

The Chaudière Falls at Ottawa, 1857

This was William Logan, first director of the Geological Survey of Canada in 1842 and the pioneer student of Canada's geology. Working for the Province of Canada (today's Ontario and Quebec), Logan travelled widely by canoe and drew Canada's first geological map – still considered astonishingly accurate. Knighted in 1856, he was the first Canadian ever inducted into the Royal Society, Britain's oldest and most prestigious scientific organization.

Beneath the waters

For centuries during the last Ice Age, most of Canada lay deep under massive layers of ice. With the gradual retreat of the ice beginning some 12,800 years ago, this area flooded and the land was covered with up to 200 metres of water. The Champlain Sea remained here for 2,000 years, then gradually receded. In those ancient days, the Champlain Sea would have just covered the Peace Tower flag. Sitting on the cliffs of what is now Gatineau Park, you would have seen whales, seals and seabirds and not much else!

① A Canadian emblem at home

A family of beavers – often used as a symbol of all things Canadian – lives on the Ottawa River at Richmond Landing, their lodge resembling a big pile of sticks and mud. If you want to see a beaver, go down in the early morning or the soft light of evening and wait quietly. ▼

③ History in stones   ▲

Walking along the escarpment below the Parliamentary Precinct, you get a great view of the sedimentary layers of limestone laid down over the ages when a sea covered this area. Hardened into rock by time and pressure, the limestone has been eroded into dramatic cliffs by the Ottawa River.

From **Your Guide**

Turn the page to learn more about the natural history of the escarpment and the work being done to protect and restore it.

IN FOCUS *Nature* then and now

Columbine

Trillium

Dog-Tooth Violet

Native wildflowers

Unlike the trees, the flowers you spot near Parliament Hill are likely to be old Canadians – for example, the trillium and wild columbine. Pioneer writer Catherine Parr Traill described the columbine in *Canadian Wild Flowers (1868)*. "In its wild state," she wrote, "it is often found growing among rocks and surface stones, where it insinuates its roots into the clefts and hollows that are filled with rich vegetable mould...." A good description of the Ottawa River escarpment.

On the river

The wet, grassy margins of the Ottawa River near the Capital offer fine nesting sites for several species of duck – notably the green-headed mallards or the red-crested mergansers. In fall, small groups of handsome, white-throated Canada geese gather on Victoria Island while preparing to migrate.

Canada Geese

◀ **Lover's Walk**

In the past, people used to stroll along Parliament Hill and down shady escarpment pathways, including one called "Lover's Walk."

A FOREST

Before 1826	1826 and 1839	1855-1875	1880-1910
The slope below Parliament Hill was covered with a dense mixture of conifers and deciduous trees.	The slope was cleared for the construction of the Rideau Canal and, later, for building military barracks on Parliament Hill.	Coniferous species regenerated to the north. However, a second clear-cutting took place alongside the Rideau Canal during construction of the Parliament Buildings.	Deciduous trees with pockets of conifers regenerated on the slope.

ापन

Parliament Hill is a Canadian landmark, and the wooded escarpment below it is protected as a national symbol

Restoring the Escarpment

In days gone by, the banks of the Ottawa River – including the slope below Parliament Hill – would have been covered with a dense, virgin forest. History intervened, and successive waves of building stripped the slope of wood. What came in afterwards was an unruly growth of a few strong, aggressive trees that grew quickly in disturbed soil. They prevented the return of native species and cast a dense shade that killed ground cover and caused soil erosion. The result has been gradually fewer and fewer species and the disappearance of conifers. A major rehabilitation project is now underway to restore the escarpment to its natural state. See the display at the top of the Rideau Canal Entrance Locks.

Conifers

White/Red Pine

Eastern Hemlock

White Cedar

NOW

Invasive trees

Sugar Maple

Yellow Birch

BEFORE 1800

Hardwoods

Beech

Red Maple

Manitoba Maple

Norway Maple

Buckthorn

TIMELINE

1930-1970	1983-1987	1994	1999
Deciduous trees covered almost the entire slope, with invasive species coming to predominate.	Over 160,000 plants were dug into the slope, and stop logs and nylon netting were installed to halt erosion.	"Soil bio-engineering" techniques were used to stabilize part of the east slope that failed due to a broken storm sewer.	Following severe damage caused by the Ice Storm on the east slope, careful planting will re-establish the natural forest cover.

Birth of a City

④Rideau Canal

The cutting of a great canal through the wilderness brought settlers to the south shore of the Ottawa River

The Rideau Canal, Entrance Locks, 1839

Into the wilderness

In 1826, Lieutenant-Colonel John By was a veteran engineer who had built canals in Canada 20 years earlier and later served against Napoleon. This time, he faced the challenge of his life – to link nearly 200 kilometres of river and lake with a series of man-made channels and to build a military supply route through a dense wilderness of rock, forest and swamp.

Canada itself was at issue. During the War of 1812-14, if the Americans had moved on that vulnerable section of the St. Lawrence River that runs along the border, Canada would probably be part of the United States today. After the war, the British decided to secure the west by building a protected supply route from the Ottawa River to Lake Ontario.

"Zeal and devotion"

When John By returned to England in 1832, having completed what many called the engineering feat of the age, he expected a knighthood. What he got instead was the public humiliation of an enquiry into over-spending on the Canal. Feeling bitter and ill-used, he retired to the country and died shortly afterwards at the age of 53. The words on his tombstone blame his early death on the hardships he suffered in the Canadian wilderness and to "his indefatigable zeal and devotion in the service of his King and country, in Upper Canada."

"First Camp, Bytown", 1826, attributed to Colonel John By (detail)

Cutting through the forest

The Rideau Canal was cut through a wilderness of forest, rock and swamp. Workers on the canal included two companies of Royal Sappers and Miners (a regiment specializing in military engineering), as well as skilled stonemasons contracted in Canada and a host of labourers (mostly Irish and French-Canadian). Death tolls from disease – including malaria – were high and the misery was compounded by insects and brutal temperatures.

⑤ Bytown on the Ottawa

The Commissariat (1827), used as offices during the building of the Canal, is the oldest building still remaining from old Bytown. Used first as a nickname for the military encampment, "Bytown" was later applied to the community that mushroomed up around the Rideau Canal. In 1855, citizens anxious to find a more dignified name for a potential Capital, chose "Ottawa" instead.

Commissariat, west facade

Ottawa, 1865

Rideau Canal
National Historic Site

A Living Landmark

A canal with three lives

The Rideau Canal is the oldest continuously operating canal in North America. Though built by the British government in the 1830s to secure its grip on Upper Canada and considered an engineering marvel at the time, the canal was never really used for military purposes. Instead, it quickly evolved into a commercial shipping artery between Ottawa and Lake Ontario. The paddlewheelers are long gone today, and the canal has been reincarnated yet again as a beautiful and interesting recreational boating channel.

The Ottawa Locks

If it hadn't been for Colonel By, the Rideau Canal might have been built like the small canals of England, with each of its 45 locks measuring less than eight feet from side to side, large enough for military barges but too small for steamboats. However, Colonel By had his eyes firmly fixed on the future and fought for permission to build locks that would be big enough for commercial traffic. He got his way. The locks were built at 134 feet long by 33 feet wide, and the Rideau Canal was put on the map.

Monument to courage

Parks Canada manages the Rideau Canal as one of Canada's
National Historic Sites. Canadian waterways are landmarks
to the hardiness and determination of their builders, people
who laboured in dreadful conditions, with only hand tools,
to carve channels out of solid rock and to build masonry
locks and dams in the worst of Canada's heat and cold.
Canals played a vital role in the early defence of the
country, in transportation and trade, and they are rightly
preserved as part of our heritage.

History with personality

The Bytown Museum, which is housed in Ottawa's oldest
existing building, has managed to preserve many artifacts of
the town's early years. The museum features a host of
precious relics, many of them donated by the descendants
of the region's original settlers – for example, a red military
coat worn by an officer who worked on the canal, a chair
that Colonel By sat in and the homely implements of many
pioneer homes. These everyday objects bring us into contact
with a very human past.

Window in time

The Ottawa Locks have been the centre of canal routine for
many, many years. If you want to see a scene right out of
history, go and watch the locks being operated to let water –
and boats – flow from one level to another. The lock
attendant is doing the same job that was done in 1832
and every year thereafter.

From **Your Guide**

Follow the pathway under the bridge
to an impressive flight of stairs. Take
these stairs up to the centre of
Confederation Square. Now you are
back near where **Walking Tour #1:
Governance** began. You are also at the
beginning of a new section: **Walking
Route #5: Ceremony and Celebration**.
To begin Tour #5, turn to page 80.

For a stair-free alternative, continue
along under the bridge to the pathway
at the National Arts Centre.

Victoria Island

The Chaudière Falls

are a place where the

separate threads of

Canadian history

come together in the

Capital

There is nowhere in the Capital where more of the separate threads of Canadian history come together so perfectly. Though the imprint of industry is strong here, almost overpowering, you can still glimpse the falling water of the Chaudière Falls beneath the bridges and behind the factories. Here, where ancient travellers camped and made sacrifices to the river, settlers began to disembark in the early 1800s, followed in short order by industrialists looking for power for fledgling industries. The traces of their lives and dreams are still visible in the buildings and on the grassy slopes where people of the past piled their lumber and built their houses, shops and mills.

Ottawa, Ontario

Chaudière Bridge

Ottawa River Parkway

National Archives / National Library of Canada

Sites at a Glance

①　Chaudière Falls

②　Generating Station No. 4 (Ottawa Hydro, 1900)

③　Richmond Landing

④　Victoria Island

⑤　Ottawa Carbide Mill (1899)

⑥　Totem (Walter Harris, 1985)

⑦　Timber Chute (site of former timber slide)

⑧　The Mill (Thompson-Perkins Mill, 1842)

✪　Stairs

From Your Guide

Welcome to **Walking Tour #2: Beginnings.**

This is the place to discover the Capital's roots as a lumbering town.
View the islands from the bridge, or wander down for a first-hand glimpse.

Start:　Portage Bridge (Ontario)

Finish:　Portage Bridge (Quebec)

Time:　Half an hour

Notes:　Though not yet fully realized as a historic site, plans for the future may make this one of the Capital's most exciting destinations.

Ottawa River

Hull, Quebec

Portage Bridge

At the Chaudière Falls

① Where two worlds meet

The Chaudière Falls were always a sacred place for Canada's Aboriginal peoples. When the explorer Samuel de Champlain stopped here in 1613, he watched with fascination as his Aboriginal guides sacrificed to the river. "Having carried their

canoes to the foot of the fall...," he wrote, "one of them takes up a collection with a wooden plate into which each puts a piece of tobacco. After the collection, the plate is set down in the middle of the group and all dance about it, singing.... Then one of the chiefs makes a speech, pointing out that for years they have been accustomed to make such an offering, and that thereby they receive protection from their enemies. When he has finished, the orator takes the plate and throws the tobacco into the middle of the boiling water, and all together utter a loud whoop."

② Power from nature

The earliest recorded use of water to produce electric light took place right here in 1882. Generating Station #4, built in 1900, is part of that story. Out of sight, the river surges down under the building and moves two huge turbines (like an old-fashioned water wheel) to power two massive, century-old generators inside the building. From two stations on Victoria Island, Ottawa Hydro still provides 3 percent of Ottawa's power (worth $4 million a year). It buys the rest from Ontario Hydro.

OVER THE FALLS!

A log raft went over the falls in 1864, with the man on board leaping for the safety of a half-submerged rock just as it went over. He spent the next three days on that rock until finally Aboriginals in a canoe ventured close enough to fire him an arrow with a rope attached.

From Your Guide

If you want to get closer to history, go down the stairs near the National Archives/National Library building (see the map on page 48) and follow the path eastward to Richmond Landing. Try to imagine this long spit of land as it was in the 19th century when settlers began to arrive, with a bustling quay lined with a shop and warehouses and a tavern just up the way.

③ The Regiment arrives

In 1818, demobilized members of the British army sailed up the Ottawa and landed on a point of land that they renamed Richmond Landing after the colony's governor in chief, the Duke of Richmond. While their families pitched their tents nearby, the men started cutting a road through the forest in the direction of their proposed settlement.

STOPPING FOR REFRESHMENT

Colonel John By, commander of the Rideau Canal works (1826-32), took time to sketch the Firth Tavern on Richmond Landing. An 1879 account recalled: "Poteen and Jamaica rum, as also the beer brewed by Michael Burke, on Wellington Street, were dispensed with a liberal hand to all and sundry, by Isaac Firth...."

Timber!

Ottawa Valley Industry

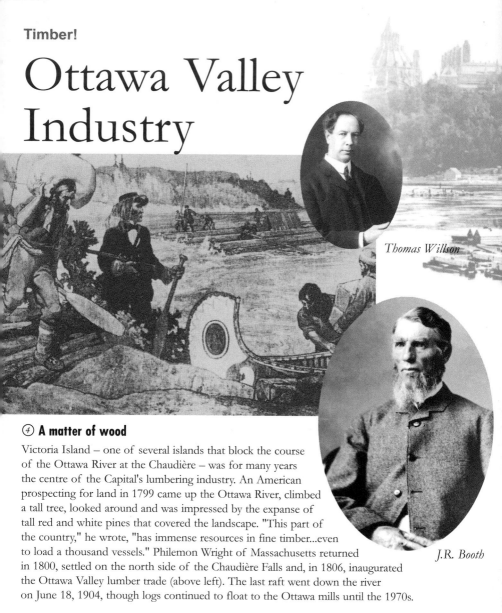

Thomas Willson

J.R. Booth

④ A matter of wood

Victoria Island – one of several islands that block the course of the Ottawa River at the Chaudière – was for many years the centre of the Capital's lumbering industry. An American prospecting for land in 1799 came up the Ottawa River, climbed a tall tree, looked around and was impressed by the expanse of tall red and white pines that covered the landscape. "This part of the country," he wrote, "has immense resources in fine timber...even to load a thousand vessels." Philemon Wright of Massachusetts returned in 1800, settled on the north side of the Chaudière Falls and, in 1806, inaugurated the Ottawa Valley lumber trade (above left). The last raft went down the river on June 18, 1904, though logs continued to float to the Ottawa mills until the 1970s.

Timber baron

The Chaudière mills were run by men like J.R. Booth (above right), described during his lifetime as, "Confident, self-opinionated and domineering in his business operations and he ruled unchallenged." Born in Quebec, Booth came to Ottawa in 1858, 25 years old and with $9 in his pocket. He rented a small shingle mill and, in 1859, won a contract to supply lumber for the new Parliament Buildings. By 1900, he controlled some 11,000 square kilometres of timber (4,247 square miles) and had 4,000 men working for him. In 1904, a magazine article estimated that he had enough timber on his limits to make a mile-wide strip right across Canada.

⑤ Manufacturing light ⭐

Thomas Leopold Willson (opposite) made industrial history at the Ottawa Carbide Mill, built in the 1890s and now in ruins. There he manufactured calcium carbide which, when lit, gave rise to acetylene, a light that was nearly 20 times brighter than gaslight.

Ruins of the Ottawa Carbide Mill

⑥ Totem

The Aboriginal peoples of Canada's West Coast kept track of family relationships and history through family crests in the shape of animals carved on "totem poles." The totem on Victoria Island, carved in the Gitskan tradition by Walter Harris of British Columbia, was raised in 1985 in a traditional pole-raising ceremony.

⑦ On a slippery slope

One of the thrills for 19th-century tourists in Ottawa – including Edward Prince of Wales in 1860 – was a ride down the timber slide (a long wooden ramp that allowed the log rafts to pass safely over the falls). A narrow chute replaced one of the three slides here in the 1970s.

From ⟩ Your Guide

This is the end of **Walking Tour #2**. If you still feel like exploring, take the pathway or stairs down from Portage Bridge. You'll find there a road and pathway that goes all around Victoria Island and also offers fine views and a picnic table. Life is great in 21st-century Canada. Turn the page to see what it was like to live and work in 19th-century Canada.

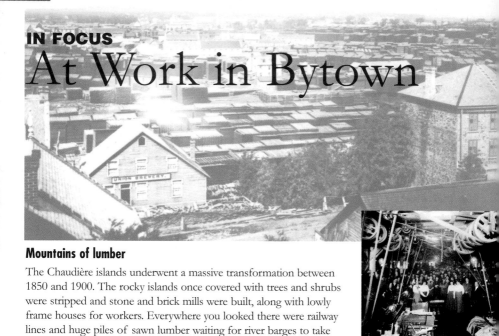

IN FOCUS
At Work in Bytown

Mountains of lumber

The Chaudière islands underwent a massive transformation between 1850 and 1900. The rocky islands once covered with trees and shrubs were stripped and stone and brick mills were built, along with lowly frame houses for workers. Everywhere you looked there were railway lines and huge piles of sawn lumber waiting for river barges to take them away.

Long days, low pay

By 1900, 5,000 men, women and children were working in mills at the Chaudière Falls. The workers' lives were hard and the rewards meagre, with people working a minimum of 60 hours a week for as little as $17 a month (this at a time when house rent ran at $8 a month and a ton of coal cost $11). In winter and times of recession, there were massive lay-offs.

On strike!

Knights of Labour on parade

In the winter of 1890-91, mill-owners cut the weekly wage by 50 cents. The result was the Capital Region's first strike, with 2,400 workers walking out. Factory-owners persuaded the police to protect loading operations during the strike, and the protest foundered. By 1892, however, the workers had organized a kind of union – called the Knights of Labour – and succeeded in negotiating better terms.

J.R.Booth and sons

Personal charity ▲

In the days before government welfare, conditions at the mill were horrendous, yet many mill-owners were personally kind men, good husbands and fathers, who treated their workers paternalistically. J.R. Booth, for example, who paid labourers very little, would order baskets of provisions and firewood for those who were ill and send his wife to visit.

Children at work

Worried about labour conditions, the government passed laws prohibiting the hiring of children younger than 12. However, it was hard to enforce the regulations. At Booth's Mill, for example, children were routinely employed, only to be hurriedly sent home if an inspector happened by. In 1872, the *Citizen* reported that a 10-year-old child had been paralyzed by a block of wood thrown from a shingling machine.

Your life in your hands

Factories in the 19th century were damp and dangerous places, even for wealthy visitors in their fur coats. The *Ottawa Free Press* reported, in 1888, that over a 30-year-period, there had been 562 fatal accidents at the E.B. Eddy mill. The mills were also full of explosive materials and unhealthy gases that caused various ills, including loss of teeth and infections of the jawbone.

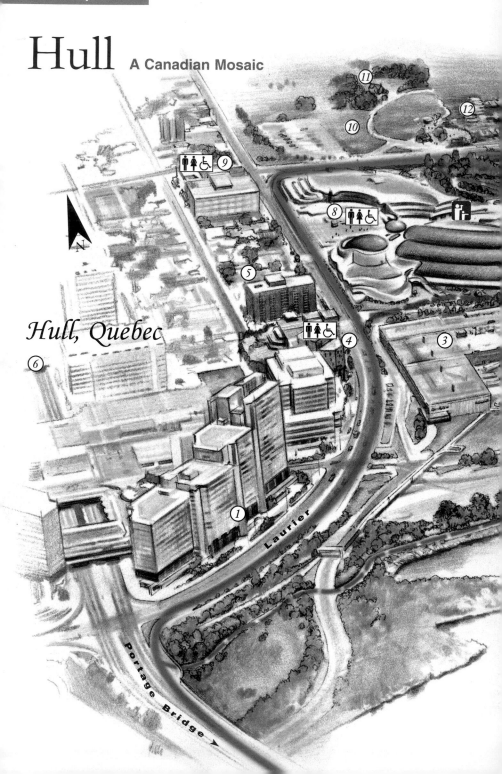

Hull A Canadian Mosaic

Hull, Quebec

Sites at a Glance

1. Portage Complex
2. Voyageur Pathway
3. Scott Paper Limited (formerly E.B. Eddy Company)
4. Maison du Citoyen (City Hall)
5. Notre-Dame Presbytery (Ramada Hotel)
6. Place Aubry (Promenade du Portage)

7. Digester Tower
8. Canadian Museum of Civilization (Children's Museum, Canadian Postal Museum)
9. La Maison du tourisme
10. Jacques-Cartier Park
11. Maison Charron
12. Hull Marina
13. Alexandra Bridge

Feel the vitality! Traditionally a place of industry, the skyline of modern Hull is dominated not by smokestacks but by the massive, flowing shapes of the Canadian Museum of Civilization where human history and culture are celebrated. The Canadian Museum of Civilization is a fitting symbol for a city that is forging a new identity as a national and international gathering place. Hull's Jacques-Cartier Park has been designated "Mile 0" of the new Trans Canada Trail. In the year 2000, waters from Canada's three oceans were transported to Jacques-Cartier Park by a seven-month national relay to inaugurate the Trail. It was a wonderful way for Hull to celebrate its bicentennial and its special place in history as the oldest settlement in the National Capital Region. With a sharpened sense of its place in the nation, Hull is also finding its place in the world as co-host, for example, of the 2001 Games of la Francophonie.

From Your Guide

Welcome to **Walking Tour #3: People.**

Get ready, as you cross over to a new city and province, to experience a different culture. Stroll along the broad esplanade of rue Laurier or, alternatively, head down to the riverbank and follow the Voyageur Pathway in the direction of the Canadian Museum of Civilization (see the map). Either way, there's plenty to see and enjoy en route.

Start: Portage Bridge (Hull)

Finish: Alexandra Bridge (Ottawa)

Time: 1-1.5 hours

Notes: Allow time to visit the Canadian Museum of Civilization.

Hull in Transition

Once a forest of smokestacks formed the Hull skyline – today it is the profile of federal government offices that defines the form and activities of the city

① Reaching across the River

The Portage Complex is a symbol of deep-reaching change in Hull. Hull has always been an industrial city and, since 1927, part of a national capital region. In 1969, at a federal-provincial conference, it was decided to integrate the Capital more fully on both sides of the Ottawa River. Within a few years, a new bridge was built to link Ottawa and Hull, and work began on a series of government buildings – the Portage Complex – that has brought many thousands of federal workers into the Quebec part of the Capital Region.

LINKING A PEOPLE, BUILDING A NATION

This exhibition celebrates the history of Public Works and Government Services Canada's service to our country. It features rare artifacts and photographs from 1841 to the present, including portraits of significant Canadians like Alexander Mackenzie, Canada's second Prime Minister – and Minister of Public Works – from 1873 until 1878.

The exhibition, located at 11 Laurier Street in Hull, is open Monday to Friday from 8:00 a.m. to 6:00 p.m.

 Public Works and Government Services Canada

Travaux publics et Services gouvernementaux Canada

 Canadä

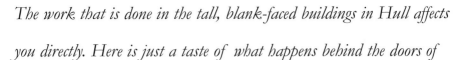

The work that is done in the tall, blank-faced buildings in Hull affects you directly. Here is just a taste of what happens behind the doors of Hull's many government buildings.

Canadian Passport Office

Everywhere you go in the world, the Canadian passport is recognized and respected. The office tower at 200 Place du Promenade is its ultimate home. The Canadian passport, thanks to international agreements negotiated by your government, will assure you safe passage through most countries in the world. The Passport Office, which has 28 issuing offices across the country, issues some 1 million passports every year.

Patents Office

Did you know that Canadians invented the electronic heart pacemaker and the electron microscope? The zipper? And, not surprisingly, the snowblower and frozen food? If you've invented a widget that's useful, new and represents a step forward, you can join the ranks of inventive Canadians. Apply to the Patents Office and, if it's truly an original idea, you'll have a clear field to develop and sell the idea for the next 20 years.

Parks Canada

Canada is still very much a wilderness country, and some of it at least will stay that way. Today, national parks occupy about 2.25 percent of all Canadian land (that's 222,283 square kilometres), and that area is still increasing. Canada has 39 national parks and reserves, and work is underway as we speak — right here in Hull — to establish another 15. Parks Canada also manages 145 National Historic Sites.

Pukaskwa National Park

Historic Hull

Forest *of* Smokestacks

③ **The Eddy Company**

E.B. Eddy

Scott Paper Limited, which purchased the White
Swan division of the E.B. Eddy Company – now Domtar –
in 1989, is one of the few relics of Hull's industrial past. A
historian once wrote that, "Hull without the E.B. Eddy Company
would be like Shakespeare's play of *Hamlet* with Hamlet left out." Ezra
Butler Eddy was an energetic American who came north as a young man, in 1851, to take
advantage of a ready source of power at the Chaudière Falls. He had little money and a lot of
determination. Gathering up discarded stubs of wood from sawmills, he manufactured matches
by hand and sold them door to door. By century's end, Eddy was
the biggest manufacturer of matches in the British Empire,
producing 30 million
matches a day and
employing thousands.

*Chaudière Bridge
after the fire*

THE GREAT FIRE OF 1900

The fire started in a defective chimney at 11 o'clock on the morning of April 26, at the
house of Mr. Kirouac on rue St-Rédempteur. Within hours, most of Hull was burning.
Six thousand people fled, some taking refuge in a surviving factory and church. Others
huddled on the shores of nearby Leamy Lake (above right) where the Canadian militia
began erecting tents the next day. Headlines across the country read, "Hull is gone!" Not
for long. The next summer, building began and Hull rose, phoenix-like, from the ashes.

④ Maison du Citoyen

Hull's city hall, with its art gallery and theatre and a
Reflecting Pool that turns into a skating rink in winter,
is part of the recent revitalization of the city.

⑤ Missionaries to the forest

A century ago, lumbermen in the
forest were visited by itinerant
priests – the Oblates who came to
Canada as missionaries in 1844
and once occupied the Presbytery
of Notre-Dame. They spent the
winter going from shanty to
shanty, helping to break the
monotony of the long winter's
work and to celebrate Mass.

From Your Guide

Get ready to visit the Canadian
Museum of Civilization, one of
Canada's premier museums. It
focuses on human culture in
Canada and abroad, now and in
the past. You can't miss it. The larger
building with many windows houses
the museum; the smaller, more
enclosed structure houses the
administration. Have a good time.

FROM HERE ⑥ PLACE AUBRY

If you are looking for some heritage charm, you should not
miss Place Aubry. A restored heritage precinct, the restaurants and summer terraces of Place Aubry encircle a
charming courtyard with fountain. Promenade du Portage,
which borders Place Aubry, is Hull's old main street.

Canadian Museum of Civilization

Peopling History

Presenting the Global Village

This is a "people" museum. As Canada's national museum of human history, its mission is to foster in Canadians a sense of their shared past, at the same time promoting understanding among various cultural groups that make up Canadian society. Although it occupies a superbly modern building, the Museum goes back in time to 1842 and the foundation of the Geological Survey of Canada. As scientists began collecting geological and archaeological materials from across Canada, a new branch was formed to cover anthropology – including archaeology and ethnology. In time, this became the Canadian Museum of Civilization. Over the years, the Museum has added other areas of specialization – notably history and folklore.

A Metis vision

This extraordinary museum building is the work of Metis architect Douglas Cardinal, who combines a wonderful feeling for nature with an amazing grasp of modern technology. Cardinal's aim is always to create buildings that look as though they have been shaped more by the forces of nature – by winds and glaciers – than by human hands.

The Grand Hall ▶

The Grand Hall is shaped like a giant canoe with tall pillars that imitate the ribs of the craft and a backdrop that takes visitors into the dark green depths of a West Coast rainforest. Here the totem poles and carved house fronts recreate the Aboriginal world of western Canada.

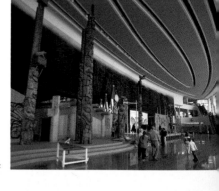

The need to communicate

Canada has come a long way since 1763, when – believe it or not – Benjamin Franklin, postmaster for all of British North America, inaugurated postal service in central Canada. Today, about 8 billion pieces of mail are handled yearly by more than 8,500 Canadian post offices. This is all part of the story told at the Canadian Postal Museum.

Join the great adventure!

The Children's Museum is all about discovery and imagination. Children are encouraged to touch, feel and experiment with different roles against an international backdrop – everything from an Asian bus to an international marketplace. And it's all hands-on! Children, in exploring over 23 permanent exhibits, ▶ learn to celebrate inter-cultural understanding.

The Canada Gallery

History isn't what happens in textbooks, but in Canadian streets and villages. While you're over in Hull, you can witness the Norse landing in what is now Newfoundland a thousand years ago, wander through a public square in old New France or window shop in Victorian Ontario.

From **Your Guide**

The red brick building across rue Laurier from the museum is home to la Maison du tourisme, a visitor centre operated by the Association touristique de l'Outaouais. Drop into this beautiful visitors' centre if you're looking for information or a washroom. Otherwise, let's continue on to Jacques-Cartier Park.

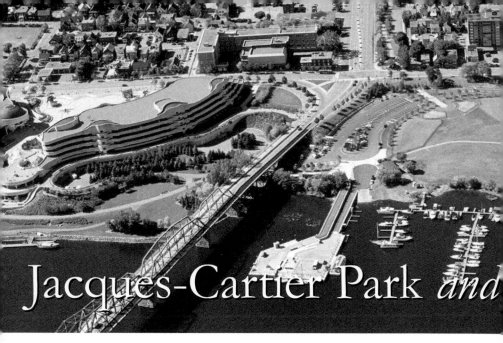

Jacques-Cartier Park *and*

⑩ Festival park

Once an Aboriginal campsite for ancient travellers on the Ottawa River, the present-day site of Jacques-Cartier Park evolved into a busy industrial site during most of the 19th and early 20th centuries. In the 1940s, the land was purchased and transformed into one of the first nationally owned parks on the Quebec shore of the Ottawa River. Today, this lovely park is the Capital Region's most important focus for children's programming during the Canada Day (July 1) and Winterlude festivities (February).

⑩ Trans Canada Trail

In the year 2000, Jacques-Cartier Park became the symbolic heart of the Trans Canada Trail project. A national relay, involving 5,000 Canadians transporting water from Canada's three oceans, terminated in the Park on September 9, 2000, in a ceremony which marked the inauguration of the Trail. This is a recreational trail system that links every province and territory in Canada and, at 15,000 kilometres (9,320 miles), is the longest trail of its kind in the world.

⑫ THE OLD BOATYARD

When steamboat travel began on the Ottawa River in 1822, the gently sloping land of the Quebec riverbank was the perfect site for a dockyard. The first of many boats built there were the *Speed* (1846) and the *Phoenix* (in the background, above, 1848). When steamboat travel on the river declined in the early 20th century, so did the boatyard. It closed in 1941, when the land was transformed into a park. Today, the old boatyard is the site of the Hull Marina.

Alexandra Bridge

⑪ Vestiges of pioneer Hull

The Maison Charron was probably built by Philemon Wright, the founder of Hull, between 1835 and 1840, as a residence for one of his river transport foremen. It is the oldest surviving building in Hull and, for a time, was headquarters to a thriving boatyard down on the banks of the Ottawa River.

⑬ Alexandra Bridge

From this fine old railway bridge (opened in 1901 and at the engineering forefront in its day), you can see much of the Capital spread out around you. Upstream, beyond Parliament Hill, lie the Chaudière Falls, gateway to Canada's interior via the Ottawa River and the Great Lakes. Downstream, many miles away and near the confluence of the Ottawa and St. Lawrence rivers, lies Montreal.

From Your Guide

It was the Ottawa River that brought life to this region in centuries past, and it is still central to the Capital experience. Turn the page to see a history of watercraft on the Ottawa River.

IN FOCUS
On the River

FROM 4000 B.C.
Aboriginal Canoes

In primeval times, the Ottawa River was part of a great trans-continental trading route. Native traders, hunters and war parties stopped at the Chaudière Falls to camp and portage their goods.

17TH TO 19TH CENTURIES
Voyageur Canoes

Every spring for nearly 300 years, brigades of huge canoes laden with trade goods (axes, iron pots, guns and ammunition) went upstream on the way to Lake Superior, returning in the fall laden with rich beaver furs.

EARLY 19TH CENTURY
Durham Boats

Settlers came up the river packed like sardines into Durham boats. Named for an 18th-century boat-builder, this hardy craft could be sailed or poled upstream. In summer, a replica is on display at the Canadian Museum of Civilization.

OTTAWA RIVER

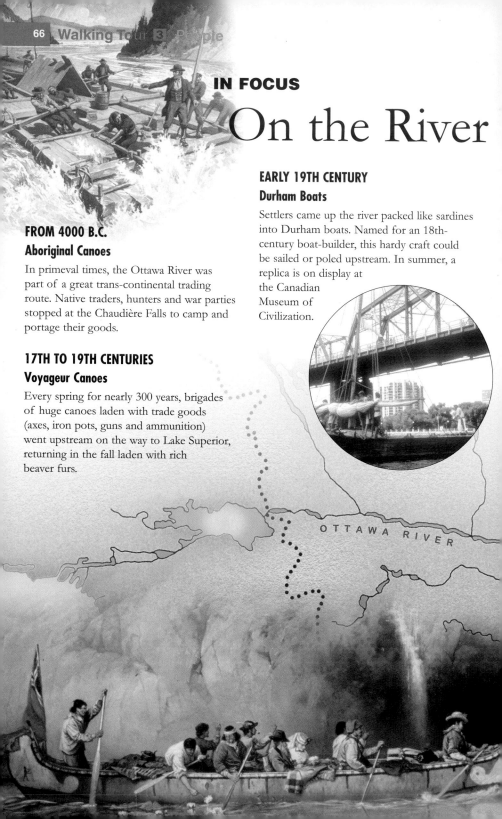

FROM 1806 TO 1904
Lumber Rafts

Faced with a wealth of trees and no way to get them to market over the falls and rapids of the Ottawa River, settler Philemon Wright devised a way of tying the logs into small rafts (cribs), which were in turn assembled into bigger rafts – almost like floating towns. These could be taken apart to float over rapids.

FROM 1822
Steamboats

The first steamboat to come up the Ottawa River was the *Union of the Ottawa* in 1822. Hardly more than a barge with engine, this humble boat heralded the era of steam travel and the building of steamboats in a boatyard on the site of today's Hull Marina.

FROM 1867
Sculls

The Ottawa Rowing Club – on the Ottawa shore below the National Gallery – is housed in the oldest wooden rowing clubhouse in North America. The club was formed in 1867, the year of Confederation, and has contributed many competitors to the Olympics.

TODAY
Cruise Boats

For the past few decades, visitors to Canada's Capital have cruised the Ottawa River in tour boats in a comfortable echo of the paddle-wheelers of yesteryear.

Sussex Drive and Confederation Square

Buildings and works of art in the Capital have important things to say about Canada, now and in the past

If you have an eye for art, you're probably heading for the National Gallery of Canada right about now. Enjoy your visit to that extraordinary building and its collections, but don't stop there. This part of Confederation Boulevard runs between Lowertown (site of many of the Capital's oldest surviving buildings) and historic Major's Hill Park, and it is rich in artistic sights. Enjoy the sculptures and some of the Capital's oldest and most fascinating buildings. They have a lot to say about how the Capital, and Canada, have developed over time.

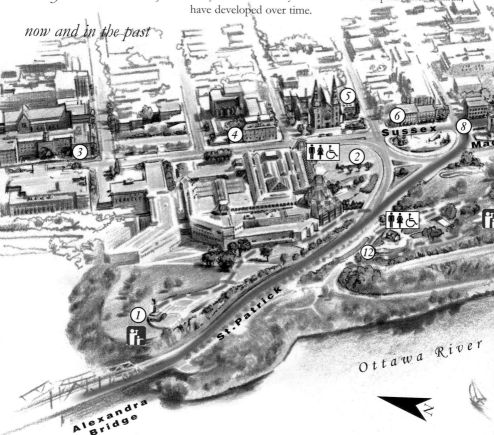

① Nepean Point (Statue of Samuel de Champlain)

② National Gallery of Canada

③ Élisabeth-Bruyère Health Centre (Mother House, Sœurs grises de la croix)

④ LaSalle Academy

⑤ Notre-Dame Cathedral Basilica

⑥ The Angel

⑦ By Ward Market

⑧ Mile of History (Sussex Drive)

⑨ Embassy of the United States of America

⑩ York Steps

⑪ Major's Hill Park

① Best viewpoint!

Don't miss Nepean Point and the statue of explorer Samuel de Champlain (unveiled in 1915). From this point of land, the whole of the Capital Region is spread out like a map below you, with every part of Confederation Boulevard clearly visible.

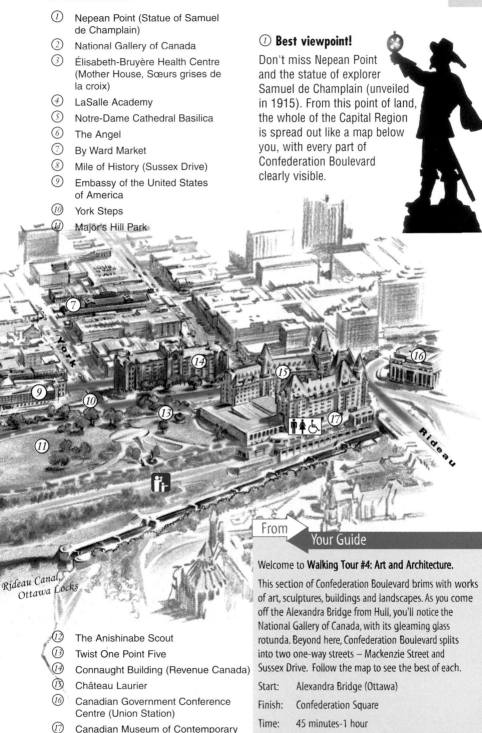

⑫ The Anishinabe Scout

⑬ Twist One Point Five

⑭ Connaught Building (Revenue Canada)

⑮ Château Laurier

⑯ Canadian Government Conference Centre (Union Station)

⑰ Canadian Museum of Contemporary Photography

From Your Guide

Welcome to **Walking Tour #4: Art and Architecture.**

This section of Confederation Boulevard brims with works of art, sculptures, buildings and landscapes. As you come off the Alexandra Bridge from Hull, you'll notice the National Gallery of Canada, with its gleaming glass rotunda. Beyond here, Confederation Boulevard splits into two one-way streets – Mackenzie Street and Sussex Drive. Follow the map to see the best of each.

Start: Alexandra Bridge (Ottawa)

Finish: Confederation Square

Time: 45 minutes-1 hour

Notes: Add some extra time to visit sites in depth.

National Gallery of Canada

Capturing Canada

② An artistic mission

In 1880, a little hotel on Sussex Street turned into an art gallery when 26 prominent Canadian artists gathered there to exhibit works. It was no ordinary exhibit. The artists – the most prestigious professionals of their age – were charter members of the Royal Canadian Academy, and they had decided to found a National Gallery. Each of the founding members agreed to deposit a work with the new Gallery. One of the first acquisitions was *Sunrise on the Saguenay* (upper left) by Lucius O'Brien. You can see it today at the National Gallery. This and other works formed the nucleus of a collection that today includes the world's largest and most comprehensive gathering of Canadian art. The National Gallery is the keeper of Canada's visual heritage and holder of a collection that spans the centuries and captures the essence of Canada's national spirit.

Cathedral of light

To walk up the long, nave-like passage to the Great Hall is an amazing visual experience, almost like entering a cathedral made of glass. Canadian architect Moshe Safdie has created an extraordinary sense of space and light in this corridor and in the lofty, glass-walled dome, where the boundary between inside and outside seems to blur and almost disappear. In the galleries also, the architect's use of light, though more muted, is equally powerful, as it is in the quiet courtyards, one of which is brightened by sunlight reflected in water. The Gallery had many temporary homes between 1880 and 1988, before coming to rest in this marvellous building. Finally, a wonderful collection has the home it deserves.

Bird Creature, Kiawak Ashoona, 1990

From the collection

A farmboy playing a harmonica, an elegant silver
ewer, a mad abstraction of rainbow colours that
literally surges across the canvas, a smooth lump
of roundly carved greenstone from the North.
As various as these works are, each represents
an aspect of the Canadian experience. Prints,
drawings, paintings, sculptures, watercolours,
photographs, works from the past, works from
today, works from Canada, Europe, Asia and
the United States – together they form the
greatest art collection in Canada and one of
the finest in the world.

Introducing art

What proud parents wouldn't like to know that
their child – having participated in a program
called *Artissimo* – is now exhibiting work at the National Gallery of Canada. This is only
one of many creative workshops and hands-on activities at the Gallery that reach out to
families and introduce children to the creative world.

From **Your Guide**

Let's head over to Sussex
Drive, past the Peacekeeping
Monument, and see why
this area is called 'The Mile
of History'.

By Ward Market in the 19th century

❼ FROM HERE By Ward Market

An exciting option! Leave Confederation
Boulevard and head down into the heart of
Lowertown. This area features some of the Capital's liveliest restaurants, bars and shops.
It is also the site of Ottawa's oldest farmers' market (1840s), and the produce still brims
in outdoor stalls from spring until harvest time. The Sussex courtyards, a series of linked
courts running parallel to Sussex Drive, are an oasis of urban refreshment. Enjoy yourself,
and imagine people who have done the same here for many, many years.

Sussex Drive ⑧

Victorian Streetscape

Mile of History

Walking along Sussex Drive, the most ceremonial part of Confederation Boulevard, you might almost imagine yourself back in the 19th century. In the 1840s and '50s, this was one of the main shopping streets in town, a favourite haunt of lumbermen looking for somewhere to spend the season's wages, and it retains much of that old commercial feel today. This is no accident. In the 1960s, when heritage preservation first began to concern Canadians, the NCC began work to restore this entire street as a monument to 19th-century commercial architecture. The result is a pleasing medley of stone and brick, enlivened by some of the most eclectic commerce in today's Capital.

Wooden signs from Sussex Drive

③ At the Sign of the Sundial

The building marked with a sundial (the city's first public clock, 1851) is the Capital's oldest hospital. In the winter of 1845, young Sister Élisabeth Bruyère and five nuns made the 36-hour trek by sleigh from Montreal to open a school and a small hospital. When typhoid struck in 1847, they hurriedly enlarged the hospital. That makeshift building later became the Ottawa General Hospital. Today it is a palliative care centre.

⑥ *Angel, artist unknown*

From Your Guide

Go up the York Steps to arrive at Mackenzie Street and the entrance to Major's Hill Park – the next stop on your tour. Alternatively, continue along Sussex Drive and cross to Mackenzie Street via Rideau.

▲ ④ Building knowledge

In 1848, French missionaries founded the Collège de Bytown (ancestor of the University of Ottawa, 1866) in this building. Today's Capital Region has four universities, but this is the oldest.

⑨ The Embassy of the United States of America ▶

The American embassy flanks the York Steps to the north. This remarkable piece of architecture, with its strong, turreted profile, was skillfully designed to harmonize with the National Gallery and the Parliament Buildings.

⑩ At the York Steps ▲

The York Steps – an exciting part of the recent development of Confederation Boulevard – are one of the Capital's newest landmarks.

⑤ House of prayer ▶

Work to replace a wooden chapel began in 1841, and Notre-Dame Cathedral Basilica was finished some years later. Inside and out, it is a fine achievement of Quebec baroque. The statue of the Madonna and Child between the spires was the work of an impoverished European sculptor who came here to compete – unsuccessfully – for a commission on Parliament Hill. He lacked the fare home until the Church gave him a commission of its own.

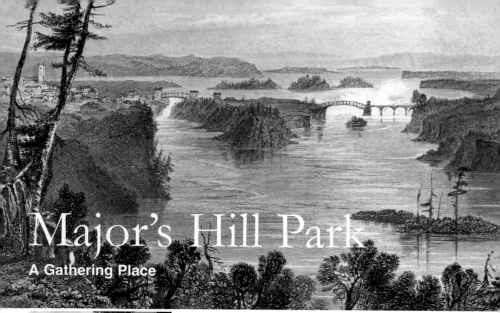

Major's Hill Park

A Gathering Place

Gazing into the past ▲

To walk through Major's Hill Park is to experience the past in an especially vivid way. Interpretive elements feature images and reproduced artefacts from every part of the Capital story – from Aboriginal travellers on the river and canal-builders all the way to the first Canada Day celebrations and beyond.

Artists in nature ▶

This oldest of Capital parks once had some 100 trees, an ornamental pond and exotic plantings spelling out slogans like "God Save the Queen." However, the park suffered

⑪ A Capital gathering place

Major's Hill Park is a key site on Confederation Boulevard. Long before it was a park, the house of Colonel John By – commander of the Rideau Canal works – stood here. Go see the ruined foundations (with interpretation) and By's statue overlooking the canal he built. After By left Canada, his house was inherited by a major (hence "Major's Hill"). This park has a long history as a gathering place. On July 1, 1867, townsfolk assembled in Major's Hill Park to celebrate Confederation around a bonfire, to hear the canon salute and the ringing of church bells and to see the fireworks. Every year on Canada Day, people come here for much the same purpose and to enjoy all kinds of performing arts, from buskers and acrobats to stilt-walkers and fire-eaters.

from its popularity and deteriorated with years of heavy use. NCC landscape architects recently rehabilitated the park, saving the remaining trees, planting new ones and laying out simpler flowerbeds and festival stages.

PIONEER ARTIST IN BYTOWN

People have been painting the view from Major's Hill Park ever since the first tree was cut during the building of the Rideau Canal. W.H. Bartlett was a typical Victorian adventurer who spent several months painting in Canada in 1838. He left us many sketches and paintings – like this one – that captured the spirit of early Canada.

Festival entertainers in one ot the Capital's foremost festival parks

⑫ The Anishinabe Scout

When explorer Samuel de Champlain travelled the Ottawa River in the early 1600s, he was helped and guided by members of the First Nations. Once part of the Hamilton MacCarthy statue of Champlain on Nepean Point, the Scout now has its own place in the Capital.

⑬ Twist One Point Five ▲

If you had been walking through this park in 1978, you would have seen artists Alex Wyse and Ken Guild at work on Twist One Point Five. Made of British Columbia fir, this work was part of a project to connect artists and art-lovers in the public spaces of the Capital.

From Your Guide

Of course, you've noticed that grand castle-like building just beyond the park. Let's go and visit the famous Château Laurier. Walk south along Mackenzie Street to arrive at the hotel's front doors. Alternatively, walk along the canalside terrace west of the hotel.

Château Laurier ⑮

The Age of Rail

A railway hotel 🍁

The Château was a capital landmark for most of the last century, and its influence on the look and feel of the Capital is enormous. The Grand Trunk Railway began building the "Shadow" in 1907, at the same time that the Canadian Pacific Railway was constructing its chain of railway hotels right across the country. In style, the Château Laurier echoes that of the late medieval period in France. That style – especially the copper roofing – was later so widely used for government buildings in Ottawa that it virtually became Canada's "national" style. An interesting footnote – the opening of the Château was delayed in 1912. Why? An order of new furniture went down with the *Titanic*!

Connecting Canadians

The Château Laurier, home to a Canadian Broadcasting Corporation studio, plays a role in connecting Canadians nation-wide. Radio has a long history at this site. On May 20, 1920, 500 people gathered at the hotel to listen as radio waves for the first time transmitted a human voice over a distance of more than 100 miles. The broadcast was effected by Ottawa's first radio station, which operated out of the Château. In 1936, the Château's radio station was absorbed into the newly formed CBC, which continues to broadcast live from the Château to this day.

⑯ SAVED FOR POSTERITY

The Canadian Government Conference Centre has been the site of some historic meetings – for example, the Canada-brokered international conference of 1997 that resulted in the widespread banning of anti-personnel landmines. In an earlier incarnation, this building was the Union Station and, with its great Classic Revival columns, it has always been an architectural monument in the Capital. The building almost bit the dust in 1966, when the railway lines were torn out of the downtown and a new station built on the outskirts. Public outcry saved it.

Canadian Museum of
Contemporary
Photography

Through a Magic Doorway

Discovering a hidden gem

It looks like a magic doorway, tall and mysterious. In fact, if you go through this door and down the stairs, you'll discover marvels. The doorway leads into the wonderful world of contemporary photography. Photography as a means of recording our lives goes back less than two centuries in time, yet even in so short a period it has changed the way we see Canada, the world and ourselves. Since 1985, the Canadian Museum of Contemporary Photography has exhibited contemporary photography in the Capital, across Canada and abroad, showing why Canadian photography has earned international acclaim, while at home it is the source of some of Canada's most stunning art.

Meet the artist

Looking for the story behind the picture? With each new exhibition, the photographers themselves take you on a special guided tour.

So what is "Photopoly"?

Simple. A game of photograph trivia specially organized for families visiting the museum. It's easy. Throw the dice and learn about photography.

Down in the tunnel ▲

The museum is actually built in an old railway tunnel that once connected Union Station to the Château Laurier. There was a time when the great steam trains actually came puffing right through this space to let off passengers at the hotel.

From Your Guide

Here you are back at Confederation Square. If you haven't yet seen the Bytown Museum or the Rideau Canal entrance locks – a National Historic Site – now's your chance. Cross to the middle of the Square and take the broad steps down to the canal. This spot also marks the beginning of **Walking Tour #5: Ceremony and Celebration.** (See page 80 to start). Before you go, turn the page for a retrospective of Capital architecture.

The Canadian Museum of Contemporary Photography houses the country's best documentary and art photography.
Lutz Dulle, Jewish Market, Toronto, 1964

FOCUS ON Buildings *in* Time

The buildings of Canada's Capital act as a timeline to show how Canada has grown, changed and matured over the years

1850s

Rachon House, 138 St. Patrick Street

Before it became a Capital in 1857, Ottawa was largely a town of small frame buildings. Settlers pouring into the Ottawa Valley in the 19th century used huge squared timbers from the white pine trade to build tiny, thick-walled cottages. This is a rare survival (beside Notre-Dame Cathedral Basilica).

1827

The Commissariat

The oldest surviving building in Ottawa, the Commissariat was a workaday building conceived with echoes of 18th-century symmetry and severity to serve as headquarters of the canal works. Look for the Commissariat at the Entrance Locks to the Rideau Canal.

1883

Langevin Block

Tastes in architecture changed and solidified as the Victorian age matured, and the heavier Italian Renaissance and French Second Empires styles prevailed over neo-Gothic (on Wellington Street, opposite the Parliament Buildings).

Parliament Buildings with the original Centre Block (1866-1916)

1914 ▶
Connaught Building

The Connaught Building – home to the Canada Customs and Revenue Agency – combines Gothic Revival, Tudor, Elizabethan and Scottish baronial styles in a typically Canadian "mix" (on Mackenzie Street).

1969
National Arts Centre

In the 1960s, Capital architecture moved away from borrowed architectural traditions and played with new forms and shapes. The inspiration for this design came from the triangular site and is based on a series of repeating triangles and hexagons (on Confederation Square). ▼

1910 ▶
Hôtel Chez Henri

Many of the houses and taverns of Hull, built after the devastating fire of 1900, feature the steep roofs, towers and dormer windows of French tradition (on Promenade du Portage in Hull). ▼

1937
Bank of Canada

Seeking a timeless look, the original designers experimented with neo-classical forms and decorations of fluted pilasters, bronze reliefs and large Grecian urns (on Wellington Street).

1989
Canadian Museum of Civilization

At the end of the 20th century, the most imaginative Capital architecture emerged from previous trends. The breathtaking design of this new museum draws on its surroundings to become a part of the living landscape. ▼

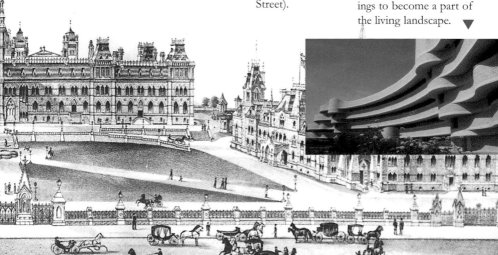

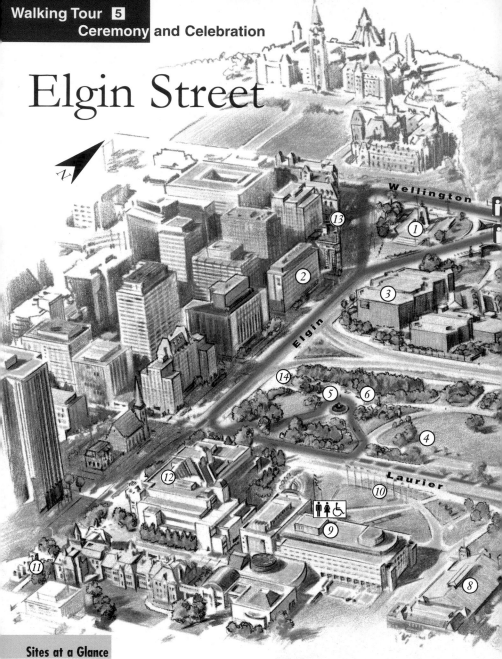

Walking Tour 5
Ceremony and Celebration

Elgin Street

Sites at a Glance

① The Response: National War Memorial
② British High Commission; embassies of Belgium and Kuwait
③ National Arts Centre
④ Confederation Park
⑤ Colonel By Fountain
⑥ Boer War Memorial
⑦ Department of National Defence

⑧ Cartier Square Drill Hall
⑨ Ottawa City Hall
⑩ Festival Plaza
⑪ Canadian Tribute to Human Rights
⑫ Government of Ontario Courthouse
⑬ Sparks Street
⑭ National Aboriginal Veterans Monument

Celebration

Whether you come to the Capital in the soft sunshine of spring, the heat of summer or the shortening days of fall, you are likely to happen on some kind of national celebration or event while you're here – perhaps something that you have seen on television, such as Canada Day on July 1 or Remembrance Day in November. In fact, throughout the year, the Capital is the site of an almost unbroken chain of nationally significant celebration and commemoration. In and around Confederation Square, there is an especially dense environment of buildings, public squares and parks that act as stages for the ceremonies and celebrations in which so much of the Canadian experience is crystallized.

Rideau Canal

⑦

From Your Guide

Welcome to **Walking Tour #5: Ceremony and Celebration.**

This route takes you down Elgin Street from Confederation Square, the same route followed daily in summer by the Governor General's Foot Guards on their way to and from Parliament Hill.

Start: Confederation Square

Finish: Laurier Street

Time: 30-45 minutes

Notes: If you're thinking about lunch, there are lots of restaurants on Sparks Street or further down Elgin Street.

Confederation Square

The Capital's Ceremonial Heart

Since 1939, Confederation Square has been a focal point in Canada's Capital and a gathering place for national celebration

Inaugurating the National War Memorial, 1939

① The National War Memorial

Standing here in 1939, you would have seen King George VI – the first reigning monarch ever to visit Canada – arriving to the sound of trumpets to inaugurate the National War Memorial. Before Confederation Square was constructed in the 1930s, an elaborate Victorian post office and hotel stood on this site. They were demolished to make way for a memorial to the 60,661 Canadians who died overseas during the First World War. After the war, there were many different visions of what the memorial should be. Some wanted a tall stone tower in the distant Gatineau Hills. Others imagined an opera house or a monument in nearby Major's Hill Park. Prime Minister Mackenzie King insisted on creating a Capital landmark for the core of the city.

AT THE 11TH HOUR ▶

The First World War ended in November 1918, at the 11th hour on the 11th day of the 11th month. Every year now, Canadians gather on November 11 at the National War Memorial. Trumpets play, prayers are read and, at 11 o'clock exactly, the crowd falls silent, and we remember.

Creating a people place

When a square was created here, two bridges were covered over and extended to form a great asphalt platform (site of some spectacular traffic jams in past years). Recent re development of Confederation Square has opened it up to pedestrians, has extended the art deco spirit of the monument to street decoration and linked the site to the Rideau Canal via a broad flight of stairs leading downward from the centre of the Square.

Brass bands and bearskins

Every day in summer, the red-coated Governor General's Foot Guards and the Canadian Grenadier Guards march up Elgin Street to the sound of drums and a brass band. These regiments have fought with honour for over a century, winning distinctions at such places as Vimy Ridge (1917) and during the Liberation of Holland (1944-45). Now part of a ceremonial tradition, they are on their way to change the guard at Parliament Hill. The regiments carry the consecrated Colours, which symbolize the unit, its history and traditions. People in uniform salute as the Colours pass, and others are expected to remove their hats.

From Your Guide

If you haven't yet seen the historic entrance locks to the Rideau Canal or visited the Bytown Museum, here's your chance. Take the stairs in the centre of the Square to find, beneath Ottawa's busy streets, eight heritage locks operating in the old-fashioned way. Or, if you're ready to move on, cross to the National Arts Centre, home to Canada's performing arts.

TOMB OF THE UNKNOWN SOLDIER

In May 2000, the remains from an unknown Canadian soldier were brought from a grave near Vimy Ridge and laid to rest at the National War Memorial. More than 2,000,000 Canadians served in uniform during the last century; over 114,000 died in service, and nearly 28,000 were denied a final, known resting place.

National ARTS Centre

THE SMELL OF GREASEPAINT

If you have ever dreamed of performing, you should seize your chance to go behind the scenes at the NAC. Backstage tours take you into a world of wonder where some of the foremost production experts in the country design wardrobes, sets, makeup and costumes and work with directors and choreographers to create on-stage magic.

A FRIENDLY FACE ▶

Architects, in planning the NAC, oriented it deliberately towards the Rideau Canal. The NAC turns a friendly open face towards the Canal, encouraging people to stop, to dine and to enjoy the waterside ambience.

③ Celebrating the performing arts

The NAC was built as a centre for the performing arts in 1969 as the realization of a longstanding national dream. Look around, and you'll see the six-sided hexagon everywhere, in the shape of the building as well as in its decoration. The architects chose this motif in the 1960s to respond to the triangular site. The image also suggests the multi-faceted nature of performing arts at the NAC, with a regular season that includes English and French theatre, orchestra and dance, as well as a year-long round-up of national and international fare ranging from Bryan Adams and opera all the way to Broadway musicals and Roch Voisine.

World-class sound

On the night of October 8, 1995, a gold-plated audience gathered in Washington to hear the National Arts Centre Orchestra play Haydn and Beethoven. It was a stellar night. Every year, the Deutsche Bank searches the world for exceptional musicians to play during the annual meeting of the International Monetary Fund. In 1995, it chose the NAC Orchestra. This small but excellent ensemble has made an international name for itself. One Viennese critic wrote: "They showed the Viennese how Beethoven should be played." Through tours, recordings, broadcasts, educational outreach and the Internet, the Orchestra and its director, Pinchas Zuckerman, bring music to hundreds of thousands of Canadians.

Connecting with Canadians

The actors might audition in Victoria, B.C., while the sets are built in St. John's, Newfoundland, and the lighting designed in Ottawa. As the country's leading co-producer of dance and theatre (English and French), the NAC partners with companies across the country to develop and promote Canada's performing arts.

Confederation Park ④ A Capital Gathering Place

The Capital's festival park

When you see the big white tents go up in this park, you'll know the fun is about to begin. Think back a few years, to 1992, when Canada celebrated its 125th anniversary. Confederation Park was the site of mass concerts that starred the likes of internationally acclaimed Céline Dion during 125 days of celebration. The festive finale was especially memorable – a 125-foot cake that crowds of happy celebrants reduced to crumbs in less than an hour. 1992 was a special year, but Confederation Park is always a prime festival site, both for national festivals such as Canada Day (July 1) and for celebrations of Canada's rich culture and heritage.

⑤ From the Old Country

This fountain – installed here in 1975 – is one of a pair that decorated London's Trafalgar Square from 1845 to 1948. It is dedicated to Lieutenant-Colonel John By, builder of the Rideau Canal and founder of Bytown (now Ottawa). Carved out of red Scottish granite, the fountain was designed by Sir Charles Barry, architect of the Westminster Parliament. Its twin stands in the grounds of the Saskatchewan Legislature in Regina.

⑭ NATIONAL ABORIGINAL VETERANS MONUMENT (NEW TO THE PARK IN 2001) ▶

During the past century, thousands of Canada's Aboriginal men and women have served with distinction in war and peacekeeping operations. This monument reflects traditional Aboriginal beliefs about honour, duty, and harmony with the environment.

A world of ice and snow

Return to Confederation Park in winter, and you'll find it transformed into a winter wonderland of carved ice. The glittering shapes of animals, mythological beasts and legends are captured every year as part of the NCC's Winterlude, an annual celebration of Canada's northern traditions and northern identity. This is Canada's greatest winter party, and ice carvers from as far away as Japan come here to take part in the Crystal Garden Ice Carving Competition. Armed with chain saws and chisels, they work their magic in full view of the public.

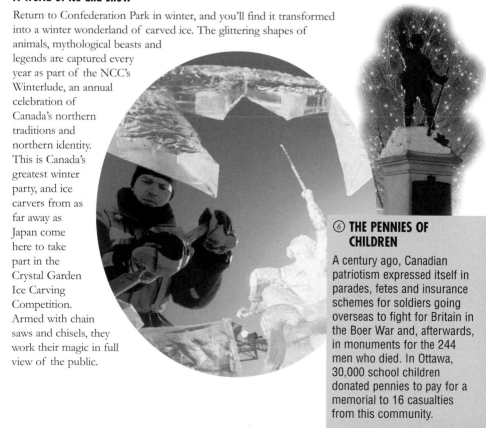

⑥ THE PENNIES OF CHILDREN

A century ago, Canadian patriotism expressed itself in parades, fetes and insurance schemes for soldiers going overseas to fight for Britain in the Boer War and, afterwards, in monuments for the 244 men who died. In Ottawa, 30,000 school children donated pennies to pay for a memorial to 16 casualties from this community.

More to discover

On Elgin Street

Elgin Street, as well as offering a grand view of the National War Memorial as a gateway to Parliament Hill, leads downward to an interesting area of small shops and restaurants.

⑦ Military headquarters

One of the things you may notice in downtown Ottawa is the number of people in uniform. The headquarters of the Canadian Armed Forces, across the Rideau Canal from Confederation Park, is a towering office complex (1974).

⑧ Cartier Square Drill Hall

This is the starting point of the daily Changing the Guard parade and the oldest armoury (1879) in Canada that is still used.

⑨ ⑩ Ottawa City Hall ▶

Festival Plaza, in front of the new Ottawa City Hall, is a place of celebration at key times of the year. During Winterlude, for example, it is an arena for snow sculptures and performing arts from all around the world.

⑪ The Canadian Tribute to Human Rights was inaugurated by the Dalai Lama in 1990. ▶

FROM HERE
Laurier House

Cross the Rideau Canal and continue along Laurier Street for 15 minutes or so, and you will come to 335 Laurier Avenue East, home to two prime ministers — Wilfrid Laurier and William Lyon Mackenzie King — at different times. The house is managed by Parks Canada as a National Historic Site and is open to the public.

IN FOCUS *Canada's Capital offers you a year-long round of festivals highlighting Canadian culture and bringing Canadians together for moments of collective celebration.*

Capital Calendar

September–October
Fall Rhapsody
A doorway opens into nature at its most radiant time of year

December–January
Christmas Lights Across Canada
Trees all along Confederation Boulevard sparkle with patterns of coloured light

July 1
Canada Day
Canadians gather in the height of summer to celebrate Canada

July
Ottawa International Jazz Festival
Summer in the Capital is as cool as the sound of jazz.

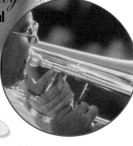

February
Winterlude
Canada celebrates its northern identity with winter artistry, music and sports

May
Canadian Tulip Festival
The tulips, originally a gift from the Dutch, symbolize peace and international friendship

Sussex Drive North

The International Capital

Canada belongs to the world, and nowhere in the Capital Region is that fact more apparent than on Sussex Drive North. The embassies, institutions and monuments that lie in this sector testify to the honourable and creative role that Canada has played in the world in war and peace. Here, professionals labour to manage Canada's foreign relationships. Scientists work to give the world such precious inventions as the electronic pacemaker. And this is Canada's "Embassy Row," home to some of the oldest and most important diplomatic missions in the Capital. See if you can spot any of the special red license plates marked "CD," for *Corps diplomatique*. These plates — a common site in the National Capital Region — are just some small signs of the Capital's connection to the world. Be sure to visit the Canada and the World Pavilion while you're in the neighbourhood.

Sites at a Glance

① Embassy of the United States of America
② Reconciliation: Peacekeeping Monument
③ Canadian War Museum
④ Royal Canadian Mint
⑤ Embassy of Japan
⑥ Embassy of Saudi Arabia
⑦ Residence of the British High Commissioner (Earnscliffe)
⑧ Lester B. Pearson Building (Department of Foreign Affairs and International Trade)
⑨ National Research Council

⑩ Canada and the World Pavilion (Rideau Falls Park)
⑪ Embassy of France
⑫ Former Ottawa City Hall
⑬ Minto Bridges
⑭ Fraser Schoolhouse
⑮ South African High Commission
⑯ 24 Sussex Drive (Official Residence of the Prime Minister)
⑰ 7 Rideau Gate (Government Guest House)
⑱ Rideau Hall (Official Residence of the Governor General of Canada)

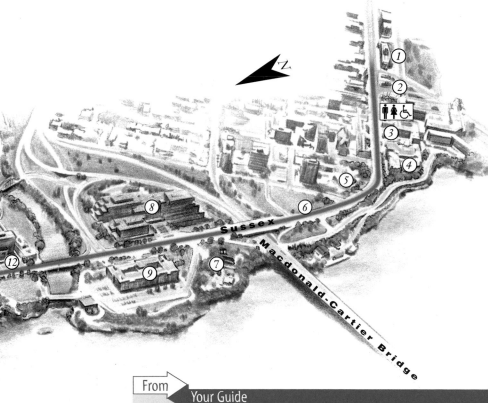

From **Your Guide**

Welcome to **Walking Tour #6: The International Capital.** This is the place to find out about Canada's international relationships. Follow this route from the Peacekeeping Monument northeastward to the Governor General's Official Residence at Rideau Hall.

Start:	Peacekeeping Monument
Finish:	Rideau Hall, Governor General's Official Residence
Time:	1-1.5 hours
Notes:	Allow additional time for walking back.

Sussex Drive North

Embassy Row

Representing the world in Canada's Capital

Today, Canada has 250 diplomatic missions in other parts of the world, and some 117 embassies in the Capital. Several of these – including the French and British delegations – have their homes on Sussex Drive North. Surprisingly, most foreign missions in the Capital are of quite recent origin. During the war, the small number of missions in Ottawa tripled with the

arrival of 15 new delegates, including that of the Soviet Union. After that, the number grew exponentially.

① Our Next Door Neighbour

The brand new Embassy of the United States of America has pride of place on Sussex Drive, as befits Canada's closest neighbour and most important trading partner.

Discover the international face of Canada – a country that faces outward to the world, a trading nation, a peace-keeper and a country of world-renowned artists, athletes and innovators

⑮ South African High Commission

For many years an international outcast because of racial apartheid, under the leadership of Nelson Mandela, South Africa returned to the international fold and is once again a member of the Commonwealth.

The first foreign missions in

Italy
Consulate General 1924

Japan
Legation 1928

United States of America
Legation 1927
Embassy 1943

China
Consulate General 1925

United Kingdom and Northern Ireland
High Commission 1928

⑦ On the "Eagle's" Cliff

Earnscliffe, the Residence of the British High Commissioner, was once owned by Canada's first prime minister, Sir John A. Macdonald. Built in 1857 to serve a family of early Ottawa industrialists, Earnscliffe was occupied by the Prime Minister from 1871 until his death 20 years later. It was purchased by the British government in 1930.

⑤ Land of the Rising Sun

The Embassy of Japan represents Canada's second most important trading partner, next to the United States. Behind the walls lies a protected Japanese garden.

⑪ Embassy of France

The Embassy of France is surely one of the most elegant structures in Canada's Capital, and its dramatic site is a fitting one. Built in the 1930s, it overlooks the Ottawa River where French explorers journeyed into an unknown world in the 17th century. The striking bronze sculpture in the garden represents *La Grande Hermine*, the ship that explorer Jacques Cartier sailed up the St. Lawrence River in 1535.

⑥ Embassy of Saudi Arabia

One of the Capital's newest embassies echoes the flat-roofed architectural styles of the Middle East.

From Your Guide

Look for embassies and their flags as you walk along Sussex Drive North towards Government House.

Canada's Capital

France
Legation 1928
Embassy 1944

Poland
Consulate General, 1931;
Legation 1942

Germany
Consulate General 1936

Argentina
Consulate General 1936
Embassy 1945

Belgium
Legation 1937
Embassy 1944

Eire
High Commission 1939

The Peacekeeping Monument

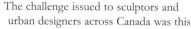

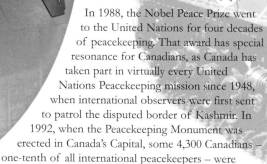

Reconciliation

RECONCILIATION

RÉCONCILIATION

The making of a monument, 1992

The challenge issued to sculptors and urban designers across Canada was this – to submit designs for a new monument in Canada's Capital – the Peacekeeping Monument. Eight teams, representing some of Canada's most prestigious artists, responded. The winner was "Reconciliation," by sculptor Jack K. Harman, urban designer Richard G. Henriquez and landscape architect Cornelia Hahn Oberlander, all of British Columbia.

The Nobel Prize for Peace ⭐

In 1988, the Nobel Peace Prize went to the United Nations for four decades of peacekeeping. That award has special resonance for Canadians, as Canada has taken part in virtually every United Nations Peacekeeping mission since 1948, when international observers were first sent to patrol the disputed border of Kashmir. In 1992, when the Peacekeeping Monument was erected in Canada's Capital, some 4,300 Canadians – one-tenth of all international peacekeepers – were serving on 15 different missions around the world.

The first peacekeeper ⭐

A Canadian – Major-General E.L.M. Burns, who led the 1st Canadian Corps in the capture of Rome in 1944 – commanded the first United Nations peacekeeping force in 1956. Loaned to the United Nations to command the Emergency Force in the Middle East from 1954-56, he was on the spot when the Suez Crisis erupted.

Canadian War
Forces that Shaped Canada

Museum ③

A litany of names

The names have powerful resonance – Vimy, Dieppe, Korea, Kosovo.... As we move from room to room, from century to century, we see the extent to which war has shaped Canada. War drew our boundaries, determined our languages, chose our bloodlines and inspired us, at last, to think of ourselves as Canadians. The Canadian War Museum, founded by the Ottawa militia in 1880 and re-created as a national museum in 1942, honours the men and women who have served and those who have died. It also tells us much of who we are and how we came to be.

The collection

Whether it's a 400-year-old helmet or the twisted metal of a gun spiked at Vimy, the objects have forceful authenticity. Along with works of art, photographs and life-sized figures posed in simulated scenes, the collection is rich in artifacts that connect us physically, emotionally, to Canada's past.

Dying for peace ★

The Peacekeeping Gallery tells the latest chapter of Canada at war with stories like this. Master Corporal Mark Isfeld was a peacekeeper with the Canadian Field Engineers whose greatest pride was saving lives. To children, the victims of war, he gave candy and "Izzy" dolls knitted by his mother. On June 21, 1994, young Mark Isfeld died while clearing out a landmine in Croatia, the one hundredth Canadian soldier to die on peacekeeping missions.

Honouring our heroes ★

Among the heroes is William Hall, third Canadian recipient of the Victoria Cross. An Able Seaman from Nova Scotia, he was decorated three times in the Crimean War (1854-56). He was also the first black sailor to receive the award.

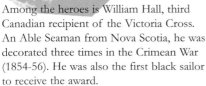

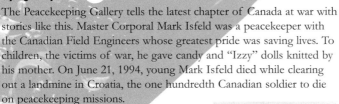

From Your Guide

Canada's role in the world is not only military. Keep going and stop in at the next building to see how Canada provides coins to the world.

Royal Canadian Mint ④

Striking Images

Coins FOR Canadians

Two hundred years ago, Canadians were so desperate for coinage they took brass buttons off their clothes and flattened them. Today, the Royal Canadian Mint – which opened in 1908 as a branch of the British Royal Mint – makes sure that does not happen. The basic mission of the Royal Canadian Mint, long since independent of Britain, is to supply coins in the right quantities at the right times and at reasonable cost to the taxpayer. Today, there is over $1 billion worth of coinage jingling in the pockets of Canadians, and this represents more than 4 million kilograms of metal. The Mint is also a big player in business, and it manufactures collector and investment coins for sale all over Canada and the world. Canadian circulation coins are produced in Winnipeg, while the Ottawa Mint specializes in gold refining and the production of collector coins.

Coins FROM Canadians 🍁

The Royal Canadian Mint produces many commemorative coins, honouring important anniversaries in Canadian life and themes as diverse as the Olympics or Canadian wildlife. Ordinarily, the designs for these award-winning numismatic coins are the work of professional artists. But not always. Looking for a memorable way to mark the Millennium, the Royal Canadian Mint went to the people of Canada in search of new designs for Canadian circulation coins. Thousands of Canadians responded with designs, and a panel of design students helped to pick the winners. The result was a remarkable set of 13 new coins – coins that mean something to Canadians – for release in 2000.

A Bear from the North 🍁

Building on the strong symbol of a Canadian loon on the $1 coin (an image that for the past decade or so has made the word "loonie" a part of the Canadian language), the Royal Canadian Mint went to the people in 1996 and asked for design ideas for the new $2 coin. The result was a beautiful bi-metal coin – the Mint has a patent on the locking process – with a polar bear image. These "toonies" will last 20 times longer than the notes they replaced.

The height of refinement

In 1982, Canada's Mint became the first ever to refine gold to 99.99 percent purity for a commercial product and to market it in its Maple Leaf bullion coins. In 1998, it made history a second time by increasing the level of purity to 99.999 percent for collector coin products.

MARKING THE MOMENT

Canada's Mint is highly respected throughout the world. In 1997, Hong Kong contracted the Royal Canadian Mint – the first time it ever strayed from the British Royal Mint – to produce a historic coin commemorating the reunion of Hong Kong and China.

From Your Guide

Continue walking east and you will arrive at the impressive Lester B. Pearson Building on the right. Want to know what happens here? Just turn the page.

Lester B. Pearson ⑧
Building

Showing the Flag

Where Canada Meets the World

Go through the doors of the Lester B. Pearson Building and into a hall festooned with over 170 different flags. These flags represent the world in which Canada lives. Over 7 million people hold Canadian passports, every year making more than 80 million trips beyond Canadian borders. The Department of Foreign Affairs and International Trade has 7,000 people – diplomats, trade specialists, policy analysts, economists and many more – working to manage Canada's relations with the world, both here in the Capital and through 250 missions in more than 180 countries. What that means in practice is that, wherever you go, whatever problems you may encounter in the world, you are never far from the Canadian flag.

Man of Peace ⭐

In 1956, Canadian Lester B. Pearson changed the world. France, Britain and Egypt were threatening to go to war over free passage through the Suez Canal. Canada's Minister of External Affairs had a better idea – the formation of an International Peacekeeping Force to work within the framework of the United Nations. Pearson won the Nobel Peace Prize in 1957.

Team Canada

Team Canada trade missions combine the efforts of the Prime Minister, 13 provincial premiers and territorial leaders, the Minister for International Trade, the mayors of major Canadian cities and approximately 300 business leaders to raise Canada's international profile and promote commercial partnerships.

COME INSIDE!

You are welcome to come in, take a tour of this wonderful building and get some insight into how the federal government manages Canada's international affairs.

See the advertisement on page 133.

Culture that is bred in the bone! ▶

The Department of Foreign Affairs and International Trade helps bring the diverse cultural achievements of Canadians — Les Ballets jazz de Montréal is only one of many it has sponsored — to world stages.

Les Ballets jazz de Montréal

On Stand-By  ▲

When Hurricane Mitch struck the Honduras, duty officers in Ottawa were among the first to know. The "Watch Office" is open 24 hours a day at the Department of Foreign Affairs and International Trade, watching for news of emergencies so that it can come to the assistance of Canadians overseas.

Fighting Landmines

Canada is a world leader in the struggle to ban deadly anti-personnel weapons. In 1997, Ottawa hosted an international conference at which 122 nations signed a historic treaty banning the use, production, trade and stockpiling of anti-personnel landmines.

From ▷ Your Guide

Do you see a palatial stone building on your left, the one that looks like Buckingham Palace? That's the National Research Council. Turn the page to find out the amazing things that are happening here.

National Research Council ⑨

Leading Canada in innovation

Improving the quality of our

In medicine...

Dr. Jack Hopps developed the technology for the **pacemaker** at NRC in the 1940s.

Dr. Saran Narang made a medical breakthrough in the 1980s when he produced **synthetic human insulin** for use by diabetics.

Dr. Harold Jennings helped develop **new vaccines** at NRC to fight the disease infant meningitis.

In space...

NRC goes onboard NASA missions with the **Space Vision System**, the technology that astronauts use to guide the Canadarm with pinpoint accuracy.

In time...

In 1958, NRC created the first **cesium beam atomic clock**, one of the most precise clocks in history. In Canada and the world, NRC time is used to set official clocks and time scales.

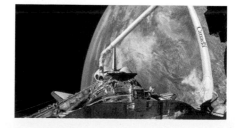

Canada's leading research and development agency

Since its founding in 1916, the National Research Council of Canada has been a leader in research. The list of achievements is long, including all kinds of discoveries in medicine and agriculture, inventions in telecommunications and crime prevention, and work to unravel the mysteries of space and time. In all these areas, NRC's research, development and innovation have benefited people in Canada and around the world. The 20th century saw enormous scientific and technological advances that have improved the quality of our lives, eradicated diseases and changed the way we work and live. Science and technology are likely to bring even more profound changes in the new millennium, and the NRC will continue to play its part.

Dr. Saran Narang

A legend and a legacy ⭐

"The sole aim of science is the glory of the human spirit," Gerhard Herzberg once said. Every story has a hero, and the National Research Council is no exception. The late Dr. Gerhard

Hugh Le Caine

Herzberg joined NRC in 1948, and there he spent nearly half a century as a distinguished research scientist, teacher, mentor and respected colleague. Dr. Herzberg discovered important tools to investigate unknown areas in astrophysics, chemistry, biology and medicine. He won a Nobel Prize in chemistry for his work in identifying molecules in space.

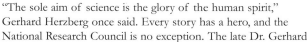

lives through innovation

In food...

NRC researchers were part of a team in the 1940s that developed a *hybrid canola plant*. Canola is used to make margarine, cooking oil, lubricants and non-polluting inks. Today, it is one of Canada's leading cash crops, worth billions annually to Canadian farmers.

In entertainment...

In 1945, NRC's *Hugh Le Caine* revolutionized sound by inventing the *music synthesizer,* an innovation that continues to shape today's music.

NRC has produced Academy Award-winning achievements in *computer animation* with software developed in the 1960s and 70s that saves animators countless hours of work.

In advanced technology...

NRC has applied *thin film technology* to combatting counterfeiting and fraud. The *optical security patch* on today's paper money and drivers' licences is made of super-thin ceramic layers that change colour in different lights.

From Your Guide

Now on to Rideau Falls Park, a fine Capital green space. Turn the page to find out about the things to see in this park (don't miss the waterfalls).

Canada and the World Pavilion

— (Rideau Falls Park)⑩

Celebrating our International Achievements

⑩ Canada and the World Pavilion

The Canada and the World Pavilion is a new tourist destination which celebrates Canadians from all walks of life who are making a difference around the world. The Pavilion brings to life Canadian international success stories in culture, sports, international cooperation, commerce and technology through interactive exhibits, indoor and outdoor programming, concerts and special events for the entire family. Located in the picturesque Rideau Falls Park, this cultural attraction is open yearly from April to October.

For more information, see the advertisement on page 136.

At the Rideau Falls

At the Rideau Falls, the waters of the Rideau River drop some 11 metres (37 feet) to join the Ottawa River. At this point, the river divides around Green Island — site of the former Ottawa City Hall — and forms two channels as it plunges over the limestone escarpment. The Rideau Falls have been a landmark on the Ottawa River from time immemorial. Passing here nearly 400 years ago, explorer Samuel de Champlain wrote admiringly of the arched falls, which French explorers named for the word "curtain." During the 19th century, mills clustered thickly around the falls.

Rideau Falls, now and in the past

⑫ Former Ottawa City Hall ▶

An award-winning building when it was first built (the square central section) in 1958, in the 1990s Ottawa's City Hall was expanded and reconceived by internationally renowned architect Moshe Safdie, who also designed the National Gallery of Canada.

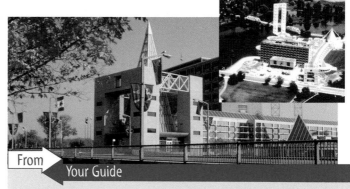

From Your Guide

Just before you get to the Prime Minister's residence, notice the little Fraser Schoolhouse to your right ⑭. Built in 1837 to house workers from the Rideau Falls mills, it became the area's first school in 1838. Also, as you pass through the gates of Rideau Hall, home to Canada's Governor General, glance to the right, toward 7 Rideau Gate ⑰. This old Ottawa house has been substantially renovated over the years to serve as a home away from home for honoured guests of the Canadian government.

KEEP YOUR EYES OPEN. ▲
⑯ 24 Sussex Drive

If you see the media clustered at the gates of 24 Sussex Drive, with cameras and microphones, then something is about to happen. Someone is about to emerge, and it may be the Prime Minister of Canada. Here, behind these sheltering trees, Canada's political leader lives during his or her term of office. Built in 1867 by a local industrialist and parliamentarian, 24 Sussex Drive was purchased by the government in 1943 and renovated as a residence for the Prime Minister. The house was originally named "Gorffwysfa," Welsh for "place of peace."

Rideau Hall

Home and Workplace of
CANADA'S GOVERNOR GENERAL

An unbroken Line

Her Excellency the Right Honourable Adrienne Clarkson is the 26th Governor General since Confederation in 1867. The Governor General stands above politics and is appointed by the Queen on the advice of the Prime Minister of Canada. The Governor General carries out the duties of Head of State, summoning Parliament, signing official documents and representing Canadians abroad. In addition to the Governor General's constitutional and parliamentary roles, he or she promotes national identity, recognizes excellence and participates in events and ceremonies across the country.

McKay's Castle

Rideau Hall, the home of every Governor General since Confederation, was built as the estate of a local, Scottish-born industrialist. Thomas McKay came here to work on the Rideau Canal in 1826 and went on to become one of Ottawa's wealthiest citizens. McKay would hardly recognize his house today. Leased in 1865 (and later purchased) for the Governor General, the original 11-room, two-storey villa has been much enlarged and altered over the years. Today, Rideau Hall is the world's most accessible Official Residence, and visitors are welcome.

Today's Governor General

Born in Hong Kong in 1939, Adrienne Clarkson and her family came to Canada in 1942 in the wake of Japanese invasion. After a distinguished career in journalism and public service, she was appointed Governor General in 1999. She is only the second woman to hold this office.

Honouring our best

The Governor General recognizes the excellence and achievements of Canadians. Do you know someone who deserves special recognition? If so, you may nominate them for any one of several honours – the Order of Canada for lifetime achievement, a Meritorious Service Decoration for an exceptional deed or activity, a Bravery Decoration or the Governor General's Caring Canadian Award for dedicated volunteerism.

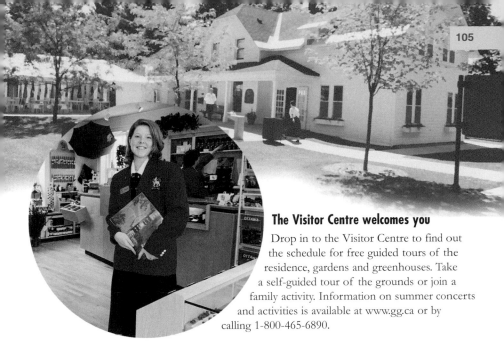

The Visitor Centre welcomes you

Drop in to the Visitor Centre to find out the schedule for free guided tours of the residence, gardens and greenhouses. Take a self-guided tour of the grounds or join a family activity. Information on summer concerts and activities is available at www.gg.ca or by calling 1-800-465-6890.

Lady Monck, wife of the first Governor General (1867-1868), in a sleigh in front of Rideau Hall.

From Your Guide

This is the end of Walking Tour #6. For more information on the park surrounding Government House, turn the page. Or, to return downtown, follow Sussex Drive back the way you came. This is also the start of Driving Tour #2. For more information on Driving Tours, turn to page 108.

⑬ Minto Bridges

Take some time to wander down behind the former Ottawa City Hall into a pleasant neighbourhood of river, park and heritage houses. These bridges were built in 1903 as the first part of a ceremonial route to link the Governor General's Official Residence to Parliament Hill. The ceremonial route later developed along Sussex Drive instead.

IN FOCUS The Grounds *of*

A verdant park

Canada's first Governor General, Lord Monck, laid out the grounds of Rideau Hall in the late 1860s. His successors have enhanced them.

Sites at a Glance

① Main Gate
② Visitor Centre and Playground
③ Canadian Heritage Rose Garden
④ Cricket Pavilion and Pitch
⑤ Formal Gardens
⑥ Greenhouses
⑦ Stables (Maple Syrup)
⑧ Skating Rink and Tobogganing Hill
⑨ Totem
⑩ Inuksuk
⑪ Rideau Hall: Government House

In the Glass House

The Greenhouses of Rideau Hall are open to the public once a year, and people file through by the thousands. Here, under about 1,100 square metres of glass, there are thousands of plants and some handsome trees, including a Buddhist pine donated by the United States to thank Canada for helping embassy staff to escape from Iran during the hostage crisis of 1980.

RIDEAU HALL

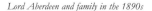

Flowers and flowered hats

The tradition of the Garden Party goes back more than a century. Once a formal invitation-only affair, the Garden Party now welcomes the public, attracting large crowds of people every year to a family day of music and activities.

Trees with names

Many of the trees were planted to commemorate the visits to Canada's Capital of royalty and heads of state who stayed at Rideau Hall.

Lord Aberdeen and family in the 1890s

Parades and pageantry

Summer sees the return of the Ceremonial Guard. In their colourful red coats and bearskin caps, they perform the traditional Relief of the Sentries outside the Main Gate and in front of Rideau Hall every hour on the hour in July and August.

The romance of winter

In the late 19th century, Governor Generals began to celebrate winter. A toboggan slide was constructed, as well as a skating rink and curling pavilion. Rideau Hall winter parties became famous in Capital society. Today, members of the public are welcome to enjoy the skating rink.

Canada's Capital Region Driving Tours

Welcome to the larger Capital – a region that stretches out over 4,715 square kilometres and encompasses large expanses of city, field and mountain. Welcome also to the sites and attractions that lie within that region. Follow our lead and head out in whatever direction takes your fancy – north, south or east – along scenic parkways to discover more of Canada's story in the Capital.

A Capital parkway

The parkways – driving for pleasure

Canada's Capital Region is penetrated throughout by a truly extraordinary system of parkways – 90 kilometres (56 miles) of scenic roadways. Virtually unspoiled by traffic lights or heavy traffic, the NCC parkways offer you driving at its most relaxing. They typically run along the banks of the region's beautiful waterways offering scenic vistas as you go. And, as well as leading you to picnic sites and lookouts, they take you to some of the most interesting and significant institutions in the Capital.

A sure sign

The roads that lead to national attractions in Canada's Capital Region are posted with symbolic pictograms. See the inside back cover for a complete key to the pictogram system.

Looking for an eco-adventure?

**CAPITAL PATHWAY
SENTIER de la CAPITAL**

As well as parkways for drivers, the National Capital Commission offers a parallel network of recreational pathways designed for hiking, cycling and rollerblading. More than 150 kilometres (93 miles) of hard-surfaced pathway lead from one end of the region to the other. From the wilds of Gatineau Park in the north down into the heart of the Greenbelt, the pathways offer you fresh air, exercise and intimate access to the Capital landscape. Bike rentals are available, and network maps can be obtained at the National Capital Commission visitor information centres.

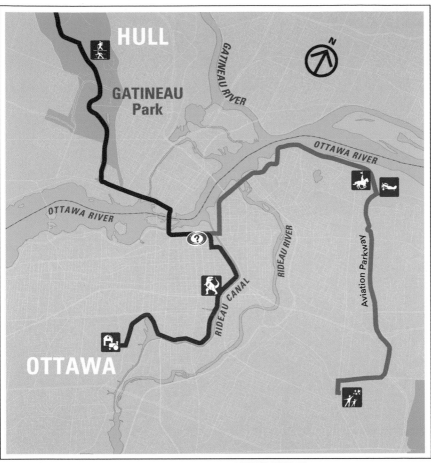

L E G E N D

**DRIVING TOUR #1:
ALONG THE RIDEAU CANAL**

Nature in the City

Capital Infocentre to Central Experimental Farm
7.3 km (4.5 miles)

 Canadian Museum of Nature

 Central Experimental Farm and Canada
Agriculture Museum

From **Your Guide**

For most of the summer, many Capital parkways are closed to vehicular traffic until noon every Sunday, and the coast is clear for recreational users.

**DRIVING TOUR #2:
OUT THE ROCKCLIFFE PARKWAY**

Builders and Innovators

Capital Infocentre to Canada Science and
Technology Museum *15 km (9.3 miles)*

 RCMP Musical Ride Centre
(Stables and Interpretive Centre)

 Canada Aviation Museum

 Canada Science and Technology
Museum

**DRIVING TOUR #3:
UP TO GATINEAU PARK**

Nature on the Capital's Doorstep

Capital Infocentre to Champlain Lookout
19 km (11.8 miles)

 Gatineau Park

Along the Rideau Canal

Green Spaces in the City

The Rideau Canal is the reason that Ottawa exists. The canal works brought floods of settlers into the region in the late 1820s, and the commerce the waterway attracted in later years kept them here. In its heyday a transportation route for steamships and barges, the Rideau Canal of today is a watery boulevard for pleasure craft and, in winter, the world's most dramatic skating rink. Today, with its banks lined on both sides with parks and parkways, the Rideau Canal offers one of the most pleasant and refreshing urban experiences in the world.

② **Lady Aberdeen Pavilion** – otherwise known as Cattle Castle – is the centrepiece of Lansdowne Park. These fairgrounds were built in 1888 on what was then the outskirts of town. The Central Canada Exhibition, held here in August, is Canada's oldest agricultural fair.

③ **Dows Lake** was a swamp before it was drained for the Rideau Canal in the 1820s; now it is a place for sailing, canoeing and strolling. Across the way (on your right) is ④ Commissioners Park, site of one of the Capital's most magnificent displays of springtime tulips and annual plantings.

The Rideau Canal Skateway ① ▲

◀ *Dows Lake Pavilion* ③   *Lady Aberdeen Pavilion* ② ▼

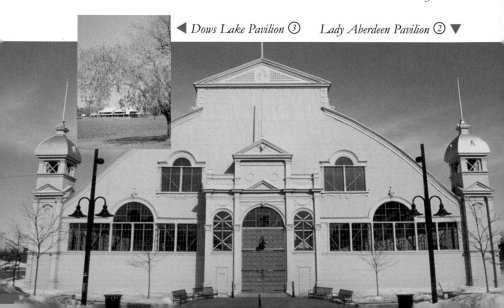

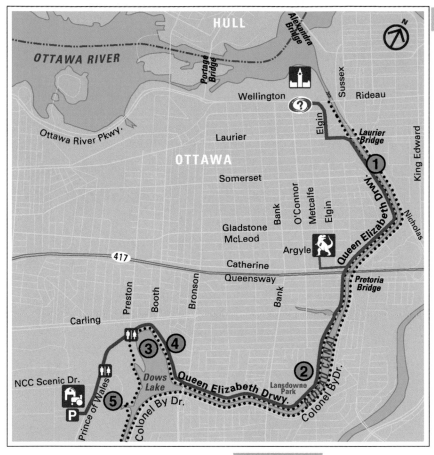

THE *Route*

Directions: Proceed east from the Capital Infocentre on Wellington. Turn right at Elgin Street, then left at Laurier Street. Bear right immediately to pick up Queen Elizabeth Driveway.

Notes: For information on Elgin Street sites, see Walking Tour #5. Plan lunch at any one of several restaurants at Dows Lake.

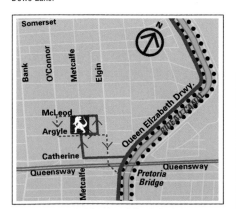

Sites at a Glance

 Canadian Museum of Nature

 Central Experimental Farm and Canada Agriculture Museum

① Rideau Canal
② Lansdowne Park
③ Dows Lake
④ Commissioners Park
⑤ Arboretum
••• Recreational Pathways

From **Your Guide**

Think about making a detour off the parkway to visit the Canadian Museum of Nature. Just before the Queensway, look for the sign for Pretoria Bridge and turn right on Catherine Street. Cross through the Elgin Street intersection (first light) and turn right at Metcalfe Street (second light). Notice a large castle-like building in front of you. This is the back of the Canadian Museum of Nature.

Canadian Museum of Nature

Discovering and Uncovering

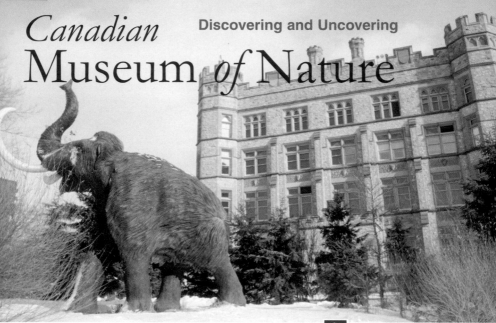

Three lifelike mammoths stand in the grounds of the Canadian Museum of Nature, bearing witness to the long and varied history of nature in this ancient land

Sharing the adventure

The dinosaurs are still what most people want to see first. In 1913, these fossilized bones helped to make the reputation of the Museum of Natural History, when an expedition came back from Alberta bearing the 70-million-year-old remains. Canada's scientists, who first penetrated the Canadian wilderness in 1842 as employees of the Geological Survey of Canada, were virtual pioneers. Year after year, they wandered into unknown territory, coming back with thousands of specimens – minerals, birds, animals and plants. For years, the collection was stored in crates and barrels until at last, in 1910, the Victoria Memorial Museum opened its magnificent doors. The mission of the Canadian Museum of Nature – a descendant of the Museum of Natural History – remains constant: to collect, conserve, research and educate.

BEHIND THE SCENES

The exhibits are just the tip of the iceberg. Behind them lie the vast collections – 10 million specimens today – and the labours of many dedicated scientists. Members of the public can, by special reservation, penetrate the world of the research scientist and tour the collections.

This is a museum that really connects with children. On weekends and all summer long, children come by the thousands, clutching a parent's hand and eager to see wonders. That big jar, for example, that apparently brims with elastic bands – it's a tape worm! At the Exploration Station, kids can embark on their own scientific adventures.

Travelling in time and space

A window opens on to the frozen tundra, the wind howls and muskoxen huddle in the muted light. Nearby, pronghorns are poised for flight across the sunlit, western plains, and the sound of birdsong pours out of an eastern forest. Impressed? Just wait. Across the hall is a garden of stone gouged from the earth and radiating every colour of the spectrum, from electric blue and thin transparent gold to hectic spinning cartwheels of raspberry red. This is the Viola MacMillan Mineral Collection, testament to a life dedicated to science and to an earth full of marvels. Keep going. The volcanoes are downstairs.

Parliamentary refuge

When fire destroyed the Centre Block in 1916, the House of Commons and Senate reconvened almost immediately at the Victoria Memorial Museum. Here, where they remained until 1920, income tax was first levied as a temporary measure (1917) and women received the vote (1918).

THE *Route*

To resume your tour: Turn left three times (on McLeod, O'Connor and Argyle streets), then right at the first traffic light to go under the Queensway (Highway 417). At the big green sign for "Queen Elizabeth Driveway," turn right. (See the lower map on page 111.)

Back on track: Keep going for several kilometres until you pass right around Dows Lake and up a hill to a traffic circle.

Watch for: Parking signs for the Agriculture Museum. The parking lot is just past the circle on the right.

Central Experimental Farm
Farm in the City

A living laboratory

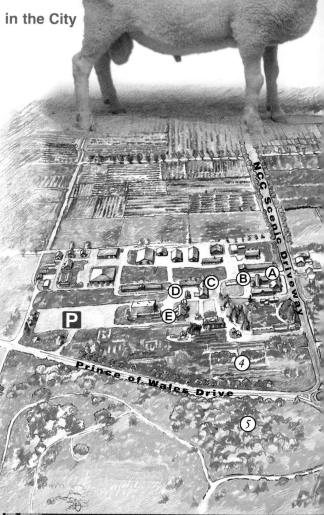

The story of Canadian agriculture is one of adaptation, as European immigrants arrived bringing animals and seeds from the Old World and struggled to turn the forests and grasslands of Canada into productive farms. Scientists at the Central Experimental Farm, established in 1886 as an arm of the Department of Agriculture (now Agriculture and Agri-Food Canada), continue to support that struggle with new knowledge, new varieties of crops and new weapons against disease and infestation. What is visible at the Farm is impressive – research fields, greenhouses, hedge collections, ornamental gardens, and an Arboretum with more than 5,000 trees. What is hidden is even more intriguing – over a hundred scientists working patiently, year after year, to collect knowledge and develop new, more disease-resistant crops.

STOREHOUSE OF KNOWLEDGE

Is greenhouse gas a national crisis? The answer may lie in a national soils database at the Central Experimental Farm. This information, along with the 16 million specimens in the insect collection – including a live tarantula – and the country's most complete fungal collection are important resources to help us make decisions.

William Saunders (right) with son Charles Saunders beside him

Made-in-Canada sheep

It looks undistinguished but, in fact, this new farm animal is a meat-producing machine that yields nearly twice as many lambs a year as other breeds. In lush New Zealand, the climate for sheep farming is rosy. Not so in Canada, where winter pushes the cost of husbandry sky-high. That changed in 1988, when the Arcotts – named for the "Animal Research Centre of Ottawa" – were registered as a breed.

From generation to generation ★ ▲

Plant breeding can take generations. Dr. William Saunders, first Director General of the Experimental Farms Branch, was a phenomenon. A professional chemist and pharmacist, he was also an entomologist who wrote the bible on fruit-eating insects, a horticulturist who created new roses and a farmer who hybridized new varieties of fruit for the Canadian climate. In Ottawa, Saunders inaugurated a plant breeding program and evaluated hundreds of potential new lines of cereals. In 1903, his son Charles Saunders selected the famous Marquis wheat and literally opened up the Canadian West to agriculture. Scientists of today continue to build on their work.

Queen Elizabeth Driveway

A rose by any other name

Canadian gardeners are forever grateful to Dr. Félicitas Svejda of Agriculture Canada, who at the Central Experimental Farm developed a rose that survives temperatures as low as -35°C. The Explorer roses – named for such hardy adventurers as Champlain and Hudson – do more than survive. They bloom lushly all summer in a range of vivid colours.

Sites at a Glance

Central Experimental Farm

① Dominion Observatory
② Hedge Collection
③ Greenhouses
④ Ornamental Gardens
⑤ Arboretum

Canada Agriculture Museum

Ⓐ Exhibits
Ⓑ Dairy Cattle Barn
Ⓒ Sheep and Swine Barn
Ⓓ Rare Breeds Barn
Ⓔ Beef Cattle and Horse Barn

From Your Guide

Now it's time to visit the Agriculture Museum. For the kids, it's a chance to see and pet the farm animals. For you, it's a chance to travel back in time to an older, rural Canada. Turn the page to find out more.

Canada Agriculture Museum

Dairy Farm in the City

A working dairy farm, right in the heart of the city, it's also a window that opens into Canada's rural past

Out in the Barn

There was a time when most people in Canada lived on farms, but farm life is a foreign experience to most of us today. At the Canada Agriculture Museum, you are invited to visit the cows, sheep, pigs, goats, horses, rabbits and chickens and rediscover Canada's agricultural heritage.

Farm rituals

The life of a working farm is shaped by seasonal rituals. At the Agriculture Museum, visitors greet the new lambs and chicks during Easter at the Farm, plunge their hands into freshly shorn wool at the Sheep-Shearing Festival in May, help to plant demonstration gardens and watch them grow all summer and, finally, at season's end, help separate wheat from chaff at the Fall Harvest Celebration.

Up in the rafters

Under the soaring wooden rafters of the Agriculture Museum barn – a classified heritage building and one of the oldest on the Central Experimental Farm – exhibits put farming in context. "Bread: The Inside Story" takes this most common and ancient of foods from seed to supermarket. The "Barn of the 1920s" shows how wheat was planted, grown and harvested in yesteryear.

Rosanne and Phoenix

Rosanne – a handsome cinnamon-coloured Limousin cow, all scarred on one side – is a cow with a story. On August 30, 1996, when fire destroyed a cattle barn at the Agriculture Museum, 57 animals were trapped in their stalls and died, including Rosanne's mother. Somehow Rosanne – only a calf at the time – managed to escape. Terribly injured, Rosanne lived to become the most famous and petted cow at the Museum. Two years after the fire, she delivered a healthy calf, named "Phoenix," for the legendary bird that is reborn in fire.

Special "Canadians"

The first settlers in Canada brought with them from France a handful of small, dark and hardy cattle. Several descendants of those "Canadienne" dairy cows now live at the Agriculture Museum, precious examples of just one of the rare and historic breeds that are preserved and displayed here.

From Your Guide

This is the end of **Driving Tour #1**. Why not return downtown along the other side of the Rideau Canal? Leaving the parking lot, turn right on Prince of Wales Drive, then left at Hog's Back Road. From the canal bridge, turn left on to a scenic parkway called Colonel By Drive. Follow the parkway all the way to the downtown. At the Rideau Street intersection, turn left to return to the Capital Infocentre.

Nestled on a **picturesque historic site**, the *Canada Agriculture Museum* is a modern, working farm where **you and your family** can relax and learn about farm animals, foods and fibres. Join us for the *Ice Cream Festival*, the *Fall Harvest Celebration* and tour the **delectable exhibit** *"Bread: The Inside Story"*.

(613) 991-3044   www.agriculture.nmstc.ca   **FREE PARKING**

Out the Rockcliffe Parkway
Builders and Innovators

With leading edge research in areas that range from heart transplant surgery to space technology, Canadians are forging a new kind of future for themselves and their global partners. To see this facet of Canadian life in the Capital, head eastward, to the Canada Aviation Museum, then out to the Canada Science and Technology Museum. You will find much to inspire you en route.

The *Route*

Start: Capital Infocentre, 90 Wellington Street (across from Parliament Hill)

Directions: Drive east on Wellington past the Château Laurier and turn left on Sussex Drive. Stay on Sussex until you pass the white gatehouse at Rideau Hall. Bear left at the first fork on to the Rockcliffe Parkway.

Notes: For information on Sussex Drive, see Walking Tours #4 and #6. Plan a picnic in Rockcliffe Park or by the side of the Ottawa River or lunch at a museum.

Sites at a Glance

RCMP Musical Ride Centre (Stables and Interpretive Centre)

Canada Aviation Museum

Canada Science and Technology Museum

1. Rockcliffe Park
2. Rockcliffe Park Village
3. Rockcliffe Lookout
4. The Rockeries
5. Canada Mortgage and Housing Corporation

• • • Recreational pathways

① Rockcliffe Park has been preserved as a green space from the late 1800s.

② Rockcliffe Park Village stands on the cliffs to your right. One old Rockcliffe house – Stornoway – is now the Official Residence of the Leader of the Opposition. ▼

③ From Rockcliffe Lookout, you can see across the Ottawa River to Quebec.

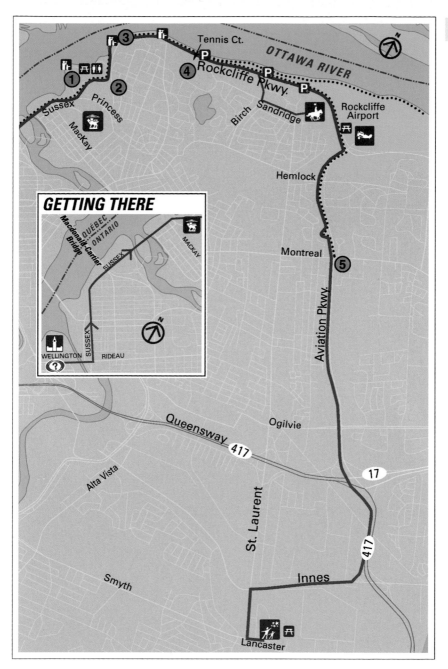

Welcome to **Driving Tour #2: Builders and Innovators.**

Not far from the Rockcliffe Lookout, keep an eye open for the RCMP stables — a must-see on your tour! Here, you can visit the Musical Ride Interpretive Centre, Stables and Boutique or take a tour (available daily). On the July 1st weekend, the Musical Ride and Sunset Ceremony are usually performed on the grounds. For more information, see ad on page 135.

Royal Canadian Mounted Police

A Canadian Tradition

Visit the home of the world-famous Royal Canadian Mounted Police Musical Ride.

Into the "Great Lone Land"

It was an awful journey. For three months, they moved westward through the featureless plains, sometimes wading through mud, sometimes huddling in the shelter of wagons as violent storms stampeded the horses. Three hundred mounted men, all clad in military scarlet, moved out of camp in Manitoba on July 8, 1874. As the weeks passed, the bright tunics disintegrated and the horses began to stagger with exhaustion. But they got there, to the western hills where murderous traders were selling an explosive mixture of cheap whiskey, tobacco and red pepper to Aboriginals. As the North-West Mounted Police moved in, the traders melted away towards the border. The Mounties brought law and order to the west, they built their forts and a tradition of dedicated service to the people of Canada.

FIT FOR ROYALTY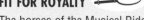

The horses of the Musical Ride are a special breed raised not far away, at the RCMP farm in Pakenham, Ontario. The blood of Thoroughbreds (for speed and spirit) and Hanoverians (for calm and strength) mingles in them, giving them their glossy black coats and dark intelligent eyes. They come to the Ottawa stables as adolescents and here, like the police officers, they go to school and are patiently, calmly taught to behave like the equine aristocrats they are. These are horses fit for a queen, and over the years Canada has presented three – Burmese, Centenial and James – to Queen Elizabeth.

A modern service ⭐

Today's RCMP supports criminal investigations across Canada with computerized data, split-second fingerprint recognition and state-of-the-art forensic science. Working out of six laboratories across Canada, RCMP scientists investigate the physical evidence of crime.

Larger than life 🍁

The third officer to sign up for the new force in 1873, Sam Steele faced down hooligans in the west, then turned north, in 1898, to impose his larger-than-life personality on the rowdies of the Yukon Gold Rush. Steele's legacy of honesty, fairness and strength continues to inspire the RCMP.

A force in the world

The peacekeeping tradition of 1874 is still alive, with some 70 members of the RCMP serving overseas today, helping to investigate war crimes in Kosovo, for example, or working with local police to bring state-of-the-art policing to strife-ridden places like Haiti.

From
Your Guide

Having fun so far? There's more in store at the Canada Aviation Museum, just down the road. Follow the Rockcliffe Parkway to the junction with the Aviation Parkway and turn left. Read on to learn about Canada's place in the sky.

Canada Aviation Museum

The Story of Flight

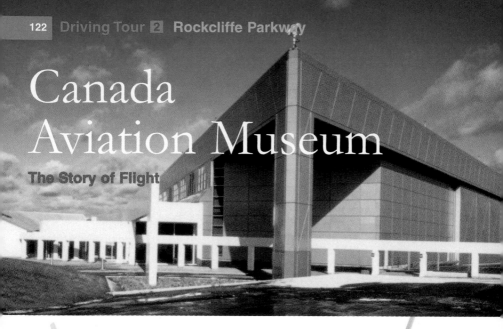

A museum celebrating the age-old dream of taking to the skies — and Canada's part in realizing that dream

Taking to the skies

People have always dreamed of flight — as the statue of the winged man at the entrance reminds us. In this century, we finally took to the skies. The original Canada Aviation Museum opened its doors at Uplands airport in 1960. Later, its collection merged with that of the Royal Canadian Air Force and the Canadian War Museum. The mingling of these collections, followed by years of selective acquisitions, has given rise to what is now the world's finest collection of airplanes. Among the 125 aircraft in the collection, there are many rare flying machines – the A.E.G.G. IV, for example, the only twin-engined German plane in existence from the First World War. The Canada Aviation Museum collects and restores the airplanes and uses them — along with art, films, models, and simulations — to tell the heroic tale of flight in Canada.

FOR KIDS... Or for anybody who has wondered what it's like to land an airplane. Sit in a simulation cockpit and see the landing strip appear below you as you come in to land with the sea on all sides at Singapore and at other famous airports.

The first visitor

The airplanes in this high-ceilinged hall look like giant, colourful toys, though they range in size from a huge Lancaster to a replica of the Silver Dart (a cross between a bicycle and dragon fly). Some of these airplanes stir powerful emotions. In 1988, just as the new museum building was about to open, a visitor arrived from England to see one airplane in particular – the Lancaster – in which he had once served. He arrived a day early, but they unlocked the doors anyway and took him on his own private journey into the past. Weeks later, his widow wrote to thank them; he had died.

Every aircraft has a story

An airplane of the Laurentide Air Service, the Curtiss HS-2L, went down in a lake in

1922 and lay hidden in the waters for 47 years. The airplane was found, reconstructed with original pieces and is now on display. A brilliant diorama shows the salvage raft floating on the bright surface of the lake where the HS-2L crashed, while divers work in the muted light below.

THE *Route*

Airplanes are just part of Canada's contribution to technology. To visit the Canada Science and Technology Museum:

Pick up the Aviation Parkway again and head south for several kilometres to Highway 417.

Exit at Innes Road and turn right on Innes Road West.

Turn left at the third light on St. Laurent Boulevard.

Look for the red and white lighthouse to your left. Turn left on to Lancaster Road, and you're home free.

From Your Guide

Keep an eye out for the Canada Mortgage and Housing Corporation along the Aviation Parkway as you cross Montreal Road.

Canada Science and Technology Museum

Hands-on History

The great grand-daddy car

When Seth Taylor invented his steam-powered automobile in 1867 – the first car ever built in Canada – people didn't take it seriously. Certainly, they didn't foresee the impact that this strange, noisy, puffing vehicle would have on the way we live. Today, Taylor's car is one of over 75 automobiles in the collection of the Museum of Science and Technology and one of 400,000 artifacts covering everything from farm implements and fishing boats to computers and space vehicles. The museum uses these objects and exhibits on the pure sciences to show how Canada has changed over time. Founded in 1967 – appropriately enough, on the centennial of Taylor's weird invention – the museum highlights an important part of our history. It also throws an interested glance forward to see where we go from here.

A museum where you are literally urged to push the buttons and make things work!

CANADA SCIENCE AND TECHNOLOGY MUSEUM

Join us on a voyage of discovery through the world of science and technology. From atoms to outer space, our dynamic scientific demonstrations, exhibits and special activities boldly take you where you've never gone before.

Let curiosity be your guide...

Discover a heritage rich in innovation!

(613) 991-3044
www.science-tech.nmstc.ca

FREE PARKING

Sharing knowledge

This is more than a museum. It's a research centre, where work is constantly ongoing to enrich the collection and renew the exhibits. The Museum has one of the best scientific and technological libraries in Canada. Scholars come from all over Canada to work here, and queries are fielded from as far away as Africa.

Stars in our eyes

In 1905, a 15-inch telescope was installed in the Dominion Observatory, where it connected Canada to the stars until 1958. Still the country's largest refracting telescope, it was brought to the Museum in 1974 and is now the centre of an astronomy program that opens our eyes to the great mysteries of the skies.

◄ Hear the whistle blow

What is it about steam locomotives? In Canada, they retired officially from the tracks in the 1960s, but still – wherever a rare locomotive is seen puffing its way down the line – crowds of people stop to look. At this museum, they do more than look. In the grounds, they can clamber on the Canadian National 6200, a giant weighing 302,823 kilograms (667,599 pounds) or take a ride in the little Shay Locomotive, a relic of lumbering days, first manufactured in 1880. The Shay has been restored and operates, Sundays and Wednesdays in July and August, out of a tiny replica train station.

A radar dish, a rocket, and a lighthouse are just three of the attractions in the museum grounds.

From
Your Guide

This is the end of **Driving Tour #2**. If you want to head back by the fast route, go back down Innes to Highway 417 and head west to Ottawa. Follow the signs to downtown.

Up to Gatineau Park

Nature on the Capital's Doorstep

Tree Frog

Think of Gatineau Park as a giant wedge of high, rocky land — part of the Canadian Shield — with the narrow end penetrating right into the City of Hull. A natural conservation area, the NCC's Gatineau Park balances protection of wildlife and habitat with wonderful year-round opportunities for outdoor recreation (swimming, boating, hiking, cycling, camping, spelunking and cross-country skiing). Drive through the Park and stop at some of the marvelous lookouts for dramatic views of the Ottawa Valley.

A 160-kilometre (100-mile) trail system leads hikers, mountain bikers and skiers into the forests and up the hillsides of Gatineau Park.

Large parts of Gatineau Park are preserved as accessible wilderness, where park managers work to balance public use and protection of wildlife and habitat.

In the 1950s, Canada shrugged off Depression and war, and work began on a series of scenic parkways that would eventually open the glorious hinterland of the Gatineau Hills to over a million visitors a year.

Barred Owl

Sites at a Glance

Gatineau Park

① Park Entrance
② Pink Lake
③ Meech Lake
④ Champlain Lookout
⑤ Mackenzie King Estate

[?] Gatineau Park Visitor Centre
[?] Gatineau Park Welcoming Area
• • • Recreational pathways

The Route

Start and finish: Capital Infocentre, Wellington Street at Metcalfe

Directions: Cross to Hull via the Portage Bridge, turn left on rue Laurier (which soon becomes boulevard Taché). Continue for just over 2 kilometres (1.25 miles) until you see the large sign for "Gatineau Park" on your right.

Time: 3 hours minimum

Notes: Pack a picnic, bathing suit, sunscreen and (from mid-May to mid-June) mosquito repellent or, if you are an energetic sort, your hiking boots or mountain bike.

Information, inspiration and insight

Not far from the Gatineau Park Gateway, you'll see the Gatineau Park Welcoming Area (see map). Here, you can get maps and brochures for your day in the park. Fairly early in the day, you should also make a point of stopping at the Gatineau Park Visitor Centre (see map). Here, you can learn about the history of Gatineau Park, encounter some of the park wildlife, and decide whether it's scenery, recreation, adventure or history that you want to see. Gatineau Park has it all.

Gatineau Park

Echoes of Wilderness

Saved from environmental ruin in the 1930s by public outcry, Gatineau Park today is an accessible fragment of the great Canadian wilderness

Saved for posterity

The idea that Canada's Capital Region should include areas of protected wilderness is as old as the century. Nothing happened, however, until the Depression, when woodcutters began to strip the Gatineau Hills of trees. Concerned citizens – many of them skiers and cottagers – formed the Federal Woodlands Preservation League and fought back. Prime Minister Mackenzie King – himself a cottage-owner – spoke passionately to Parliament. "Whole hillsides...have been completely denuded of their trees," he said. "There have been left devastated areas which are nothing else but barren rocks and eroded soil.... Streams and springs are drying up, and the wild life of the woods and waters disappearing." In 1938, the government purchased the first few properties for what is now Gatineau Park, today measuring 35,600 hectares (88,000 acres) and managed by the NCC.

④ CHAMPLAIN LOOKOUT

Nowhere is the division between Canadian Shield to the north and St. Lawrence Lowlands to the south more dramatically visible than from here, atop the Eardley Escarpment, where the steep shoulder of Gatineau Park rises over the Ottawa Valley.

A haunted landscape

As you drive, notice clearings along the way where rocks are piled and old fence rails lie half collapsed. These were farmsteads once, places where poor settlers came in the early 19th century and tried to force a living out of the harsh, stony ground. One by one, they abandoned their farms to nature.

② Prehistoric relics

Pink Lake is a rare "meromictic" lake. Small but deep, the lake has no circulation in its depths, no oxygen and no decomposition. Pink Lake is thus a veritable treasure house of ancient life forms, pollen and bacteria. Once a favourite destination for picnickers and swimmers in summer, Pink Lake was almost destroyed by heavy traffic. It has been restored now, the banks have been replanted to prevent erosion and to protect this natural treasure. Stop at the lookout and learn more or, a little further, park and walk around the lake on an interpretation trail.

From Your Guide

Gatineau Park offers more than landscape and recreation. If you want to do a little time travel, stop off at the Mackenzie King Estate, the restored country home of Canada's longest serving prime minister. Try the Tea Room for lunch.

③ MEECH LAKE

There are pockets of private property in the park, as in the cottages that line Meech Lake, which is also the site of two public beaches as well. The government conference centre at this lake was the site of the Meech Lake Accord of 1990.

Mackenzie King
Estate ⑤

Legacy to Canadians

His gift to the Canadian people was a fragment of the Canadian wilderness to be preserved forever on their behalf

A present to his country

During a career in politics that spanned a half century, Mackenzie King, Canada's longest serving prime minister, spent every hour he could at his country estate in the Gatineau Hills. For 50 years, he summered and entertained his friends there. In the 1930s, he campaigned for the creation of a park that would preserve those beloved hills from devastation. When he died in 1950, he bequeathed his land to the Canadian people as the core of what is now Gatineau Park. "I had not been long in office," he wrote in his will, "before I conceived the idea of acquiring sufficient land to make the Kingsmere properties into a park...which some day I might present to my country...."

THE FARM

Notice the white frame building near the entrance to the Mackenzie King Estate. This is The Farm. In the last years of his life, King purchased an old farmstead and turned it into a year-round show-piece. The Farm, which is not open to the public, is now the Official Residence of the Speaker of the House of Commons.

Mackenzie King at The Farm, 1950

Love at First Sight

The year was 1900. Mackenzie King was a young man then, an expert in labour relations recently hired by the federal civil service. One Thanksgiving, he happened to cycle up into the Gatineau Hills and fell in love. For the rest of his life, the Gatineau Hills were King's refuge, a place to swim and canoe and walk the forest. Three years after his first visit, King purchased land on Kingsmere Lake and built a little cottage, then a second one for guests (the Kingswood cottages). Later, he moved up the hill to the larger, grander Moorside. The love affair never ended.

The Abbey Ruins

Mackenzie scoured Ottawa and the world for interesting bits of stone from which to build his "ruins." He seized some from Canada's old Parliament Buildings – destroyed by fire in 1916 – and even begged a few from London after the Blitz.

From Your Guide

This is the end of Driving Tour #3. You can head back to the city the way you came or, as the map shows, by Highway 5. But the adventure doesn't have to end here. So far, you've explored only about one-third of the park. Armed with a map and swimming gear, why not keep going – to Lac Philippe or Lac Lapêche – to enjoy the beaches or rent a canoe.

THE GARDEN

Old photographs show King in the garden at Moorside, often with his beloved dog, Pat. A few years ago, those gardens were restored to their old shape, with the same varieties of plants that grew here when King was in residence.

Department of Foreign Affairs
and International Trade

Ministère des Affaires étrangères
et du Commerce international

Where Canada Meets the World

Guided Tours of the
Lester B. Pearson Building
125 Sussex Drive, Ottawa

Tour this important Ottawa landmark, the focal point for Canada's role in the community of nations.

See exhibits and displays highlighting the Department's activities in Canada and around the world.

Learn more about the life of Lester B. Pearson, Canada's most distinguished statesman.

View an impressive collection of Canadian art and a permanent display of flags representing 186 countries.

Find out about the people who shape Canada's foreign and trade policy.

Bilingual tours are open to the general public.
Pre-arranged tours for groups by reservation.
All tours are free of charge.

Meetings with officers of the Department may be arranged for groups.

Please call: **(613) 992-9541**

for more information or to book a tour,
or send an e-mail to:

tours-visites@dfait-maeci.gc.ca

www.dfait-maeci.gc.ca

Canada

Currency Museum

Discover the
Currency
Museum

Step back in time and explore the
evolution of money around the world
and through the ages.

*Where
money
talks*

Bank of Canada

245 Sparks Street, Ottawa   (613) 782-8914
W W W . C U R R E N C Y M U S E U M . C A

Meet the Mounties and horses of the Musical Ride at the RCMP Musical Ride Centre

A living tribute to Canadian heritage and history

www.rcmp.ca

for general information and group bookings call:

(613) 998-8199

CREDITS

Please note: NCC = National Capital Commission   NAC = National Archives of Canada

Frontispiece

Map of Confederation Boulevard, Eugene Kral

Confederation Boulevard Walking Tours

Introduction

Page(s)

2   NCC.

3   Top, Ewald Richter/NCC; middle, P.-St. Jacques/NCC; bottom, NCC.

4   Upper left, NV/NCC; top right, NCC; middle right, NV/NCC; middle and bottom right, NCC; bottom left, NV/NCC.

5   Middle left (2 images), NCC; top right, NCC; middle right, NCC; bottom right, NCC; bottom and middle left, NV/NCC.

8   Background, CTC; bottom left, NAC, C114504; bottom right, NAC, C70249.

9   Map, Department of Canadian Heritage; bottom left, NAC, C70342; bottom right, NAC, C7885.

10   Middle (collage), CTC; bottom left, NAC, C3207; bottom middle, NAC, C61936; bottom right, NAC, C10932.

11   Collage, CTC; bottom left, NAC, PA16196; bottom middle, NAC, PA117000.

12   Top, NCC; middle left, NAC, C70673; bottom right, NAC, C13320.

13   Middle right, NAC, PA123917; bottom, NAC, C7715.

14   René Benet, Gatineau Hot Air Balloon Festival.

15   NCC.

16   Top, NCC; bottom left, DFAIT.

17   NCC.

18   NCC.

19   Top left, NV/NCC; middle left, J. Uren; others, NCC.

Walking Tour #1

20-21   Map: Eugene Kral.

22   Top. NV/NCC; middle left, NAC, C11864; bottom, NAC, C83946 (detail).

23   Top, NAC, C104616; middle left, NAC, C2498; middle right, NAC, PA 51553; bottom, NAC, RD243.

24   Top, CTC; upper middle (inset), NAC, PA151868; lower middle, CTC; bottom left and right, Department of Canadian Heritage.

25   Top right, NCC; middle left and inset, NV/NCC.

26   Top, Malak; middle and bottom, Library of Parliament.

27   Top middle and right, Library of Parliament; top middle, NAC, C7374; bottom middle, NAC, PA143969; bottom, Eleanor Milne.

28   Top, NAC, C1548; bottom left, NV/NCC.

29   NV/NCC.

30   Top, NV/NCC; bottom left, J. Uren.

31   Left, NAC, C4908; right top and bottom, NV/NCC.

32   Top, NCC; bottom, J. Uren.

33   Currency Museum.

34   NV/NCC.

35   Top, Supreme Court of Canada/Photographer: Philippe Landreville; middle, Supreme Court of Canada; bottom right, NV/NCC.

36   Background, NCC; left, NAC; middle right, NV/NCC; bottom right, NAC, C34005.

37   Top left, NAC, PA12607; middle right, National Library of Canada.

Interlude: River Walk

38-39   Map, Eugene Kral.

40   Top, NAC, C2813; bottom right, NAC, C10459.

41   Top, NV/NCC; bottom, NCC.

42   Bottom left, NAC, C82874; top right, A. Fitzgibbon, in *Canadian Wild Flowers* by C. P. Traill, 1868; middle right, NCC.

44   Top, W. H. Bartlett, 1839; middle, Royal Engineers Museum.

45   Top, McCord Museum; upper middle right, NAC, C12607; lower middle left, NCC; bottom, NAC, C1185.

46   Top, NCC; bottom, NV/NCC.

47   NCC.

Walking Tour #2

48-49   Map, Eugene Kral.

50   Top, NAC, C11848; middle, NAC, PA28221; bottom, NAC, C4620.

51   Top, *Indians Paying Homage to the Spirit of the Chaudière*, C. W. Jefferys/NAC, C73701; middle left, NAC, C5741; bottom, NAC, C226.

52   Top left, *Philemon Wright Overseeing the Descent of the First Timber Raft*, 1806, C. W. Jefferys/NAC, C003861; top right, NAC, C53499; right, NAC, PA25545.

53   Top, NAC, C5096; middle, NV/NCC; bottom, NAC, PA12560.

54   Top, NAC, PA8407; upper right, NAC, PA74697; lower right, NAC, PA103086; bottom left, NAC, PA120161.

55   Top, NAC, PA33271; middle left, NAC, C30945; bottom, NAC, PA12999.

Walking Tour #3

56-57   Map, Eugene Kral.

58   NV/NCC.

59   Bottom, Parks Canada.

60   Top, NCC; inset, NAC, PA26419; bottom left, NCC; bottom right, NAC, PA135445.

61   Top, NV/NCC; bottom, NCC.

62-63   Top and bottom, NV/NCC.

62   Centre, NCC.

63   Upper middle left, Canadian Museum of Civilization S93-14850; upper middle right, Canadian Museum of Civilzation S93-5438; lower middle left and right, Canadian Children's Museum.

64-65   Top, NCC.

64   Middle right, Trans Canada Trail Foundation; bottom right, NV/NCC.

65   Inset, NV/NCC; middle, NCC; bottom, Colin Rowe/NCC.

66   Top left, *The First Raft on the Ottawa*, 1806, C. W. Jefferys/NAC, C73702; middle, Canadian Museum of Civilization S97-10737; bottom, NAC, C12607.

67   Middle left, NCC; top right, Elmwood School; bottom right, NV/NCC.